A

Daughter of Han

THE AUTOBIOGRAPHY OF
A Chinese Working Woman

BY

IDA PRUITT

FROM THE STORY TOLD HER BY

NING LAO T'AI-T'AI

Martino Publishing
Mansfield Centre, CT
2011

Martino Publishing
P.O. Box 373,
Mansfield Centre, CT 06250 USA

www.martinopublishing.com

ISBN   978-1-61427-094-2

© *2011 Martino Publishing*

Cover design by T. Matarazzo

Printed in the United States of America On 100% Acid-Free Paper

A

Daughter of Han

THE AUTOBIOGRAPHY OF
A Chinese Working Woman

BY

IDA PRUITT

FROM THE STORY TOLD HER BY

NING LAO T'AI-T'AI

NEW HAVEN

YALE UNIVERSITY PRESS

LONDON · GEOFFREY CUMBERLEGE · OXFORD UNIVERSITY PRESS

THE PHILIP HAMILTON MCMILLAN
MEMORIAL PUBLICATION FUND

THE present volume is the thirty-fourth work published by the Yale University Press on the Philip Hamilton Mc-Millan Memorial Publication Fund. This Foundation was established December 12, 1922, by a gift to Yale University in pursuance of a pledge announced on Alumni University Day in February, 1922, of a Fund of $100,000 bequeathed to James Thayer McMillan and Alexis Caswell Angell, as Trustees, by Mrs. Elizabeth Anderson McMillan, of Detroit, to be devoted by them to the establishment of a memorial in honor of her husband.

He was born in Detroit, Michigan, December 28, 1872, prepared for college at Phillips Academy, Andover, and was graduated from Yale in the Class of 1894. As an undergraduate he was a leader in many of the college activities of his day, and within a brief period of his graduation was called upon to assume heavy responsibilities in the management and direction of numerous business enterprises in Detroit, where he was also a Trustee of the Young Men's Christian Association and of Grace Hospital. His untimely death, from heart disease, on October 4, 1919, deprived his city of one of its leading citizens and his University of one of its most loyal sons.

CONTENTS

PROLOGUE   1

THE CITY   5

BOOK ONE. THE FAMILY

I.   CHILDHOOD, 1867–1870   11

II.   GROWING UP, 1870–1881   20

III.   THE WEDDING, 1881   35

IV.   MARRIAGE, 1881–1887   39

V.   MY FATHER AND MY MOTHER, 1881–1887   48

VI.   STARVATION, 1887–1888   55

VII.   THE YOUNGER CHILD, 1889   66

BOOK TWO. IN SERVICE

VIII. WITH THE MILITARY OFFICIALS, 1889–1896   74

IX.   THE JAPANESE COME, 1895   87

X.   WITH THE MOHAMMEDANS, 1895–1897   94

XI.   WITH THE CIVIL OFFICIALS, 1897–1899   115

BOOK THREE. THE FAMILY

XII.   TOGETHER AGAIN, 1899   142

XIII. WITH THE MISSIONARIES, 1899–1902   145

XIV.	MANTZE'S MARRIAGE, 1901	153
XV.	CHILDREN AND GRANDCHILDREN, 1902–1910	163
XVI.	NEIGHBORS, 1902–1911	175
XVII.	CHEFOO, 1911–1921	195
XVIII.	MY SON IS STARTED IN LIFE, 1921–1925	218
XIX.	PEIPING, 1928–1934	229
XX.	THE FAMILY ESTABLISHED, 1934–1937	236
XXI.	THE JAPANESE COME AGAIN, 1937–1938	240

ILLUSTRATIONS

LAO T'AI T'AI TELLS HER STORY   2

FLOOR PLAN OF A THREE-CHIEN HOUSE   21

MAP SHOWING PLACES WHERE LAO T'AI T'AI LIVED AND
TRAVELED   129

LAO T'AI T'AI AND HER FAMILY   198

LAO T'AI T'AI LEARNS SOMETHING ABOUT AMERICA   238

ACKNOWLEDGEMENTS

I want to express my sincerest appreciation to Mr. Thomas Handforth for the drawing of the end-paper map in the making of which Mr. Handforth was both artist and lover of China; also to Mr. Henry S. Kelly for drawing the floor plan of the three-chien house and the map showing the places where Lao T'ai T'ai lived and visited.

PROLOGUE

ONE day I was chatting with a Chinese friend, a young matron, and asked if she knew the old customs of Chinese families in childbirth and marriage and death. She said that she did not. Her parents had lived in one of the port cities and she had been in missionary boarding school most of her life until her marriage. But she spoke of the mother of one of the men who worked for her husband, an old lady with great energy and nothing to do. She might be willing to come and tell me what I wanted to know and, in addition to the customs, she knew many of the old stories, for she spent much of her time at the fairs listening to the storytellers. It was arranged that she should come three times a week while I was having breakfast. It was the only time that I could be sure to be free.

She came. For two years she came three times a week and told me many tales and of many customs and to illustrate these customs she told me more tales until the story of her life lay before me.

We became friends so that she came not to tell me stories but because we enjoyed being together. In the spring she watched the flowers in the court come out and talked about them. In the summer she sympathized with me over the colic the puppies had. And one summer we raised silk worms, for I had two mulberry trees, but the venture was not very successful. No one had time to pick enough fresh leaves for the creatures. They were stunted in growth and made indifferent silk.

At first I would urge her to have breakfast with me but she would always say, "I have had my breakfast." It was a point of pride with her. But I soon found that an orange or a banana and a cup of coffee were not breakfast but refreshments that could be offered to a caller. Never would she take more than one cup of coffee or more than one piece of fruit, but she would smoke any number of cigarettes, so I kept the box and the ash tray by her side.

"I have had a full life. I have seen wonderful sights. I have seen the sea floating with dead bodies like gold fish in a pond when bread is thrown to them. I have seen the great of this world and have eaten the food that was prepared for them. I have suffered bitterly. I have suffered hunger and I have suffered the sight of my children sold. All have I had in a superlative degree." Then she looked down at her lap. Her square, rugged face broke into the smile that showed why we were friends. She took up the corner of her blue cotton coat, cut peasant style. "But never have I worn good clothing. I have always worn these peasant clothes. I am used to them now and cannot change."

Within the common destiny is the individual destiny. That destiny is fixed by heaven, by the stars in their courses. Only as one lives does the pattern of one's life show forth.

With her life behind her the pattern of Lao T'ai-t'ai's life is clear. She has borne children and raised them and grandchildren. The next two links in the chain are assured. She sees her grandchildren around her. Her work is done.

The gift of humor and of seeing things as they are she shares with her people. But perhaps the generous portion of both which the gods have given her were to make up for the slender share of worldly goods which has come her way. Her work is done but her life is not over.

LAO T'AI T'AI TELLS HER STORY

There are the good things of the world to enjoy when the troubles brought by the Japanese shall have passed. There are her children and her grandchildren to think for, to counsel, and to enjoy. She is now the Lao T'ai-t'ai, the Old Mistress, and life would be fair indeed if the Japanese had not come.

What they have done to her I do not like to think. I left Peiping in 1938 and have heard nothing of her since. The Japanese had been there a little over a year when I left, and the city was quiet as it had been from the first. The Japanese liked Peiping and wanted it for themselves. They never fought in the city and always maintained order.

But there is something that is worse than physical destruction. The oppression and control which are more terrible for a people than the rape and murder and opium addiction of a few were beginning when I left the city. This oppression was being accomplished in such a way that Lao T'ai-t'ai, with her direct personal point of view and simple way of living, would have had small chance of seeing and evaluating it until it had been accomplished.

Each business was becoming Japanese-controlled by the simple process of telling the owners that 50 per cent of the stock belonged to a Japanese, and of levying fines. Monopolies were being set up that would make the Chinese the bearers of burdens and the Japanese those that rode in the motor cars and the rickshas and lived in the beautiful gardens of the city. Schoolbooks were being "edited" so that the children of the city would think the "right thoughts."

The city was quiet, and people who lived as Lao T'ai-t'ai and her family lived would be among the last to feel the Japanese yoke; it would settle on them by degrees imperceptible to them. Unless they and all the others are rescued in time, they will live without freedom of soul, at best dry shells of life, like people I have seen in Japan and Korea and Manchuria, and at worst, in a slavery and destitution that make Lao T'ai-t'ai's days as a beggar seem paradise. May the black night of invasion and oppression lift in time for Lao T'ai-t'ai to enjoy a few more years of peace and see her grandchildren set out firmly and well on the road of life.

IDA PRUITT

THE CITY

P'ENGLAI stands on a rocky hill by the sea, facing Manchuria, on the peninsula of Shantung province which reaches out into the Yellow Sea toward Korea. Its walls climb and sink with the rocky ridges which stretch to the east and west and south. North of the city, beyond the strip of arable land and the sand dunes, are the ocean and the islands which stand like gigantic steppingstones to the shores of the Manchurian peninsula. Immediately west of the city the hills break into a crest capped with a beacon mound from which wolf-dung signal smoke, in times gone by, rose straight and thin and black. To the north the land falls in a sheer cliff. Perched on top of the cliff is the Temple of the Blessed Isles. It commemorates the search for those islands by the great emperor Ch'in Shih Huang Ti (221–210 B.C.), the conqueror, the tyrant, the empire unifier, the wall builder, the searcher after immortality. On the terrace of the temple, overlooking the tumbling waves, the great poet Su Tung-p'o, who was an official in the city, wrote verses which have been carved on stone and placed in the walls of the guest hall, and his statue sits there looking ever out to sea.

Below the hill, surrounding a small inlet and the houses around the inlet, is another wall. This is the Water City, the harbor for the fleet of imperial war junks and town for the semi-imperial garrison. From here, says legend, the five hundred maids and five hundred youths were dispatched on that search for the herb of immortality which ended not in long life for the Emperor but in the founding of the Japanese nation. There are tales of a mystic dolphin seen from the cliffs above, at which the mighty Emperor cast an impotent spear and knew that his days were numbered.

The gray walls of the city itself are crowned by gate towers of three stories instead of the usual two, because the uncle of the first Emperor of the Sui dynasty (A.D. 589–618) was once, when this millennium was young, prince of that territory. The gate towers float proudly above a proud city.

Between the main city of P'englai and the Water City is a moat, on either side of which there is a wide road paved with dressed stone along which iron-tired carts rumble and people walk with the soft pat of cloth-soled shoes. Many hundreds of years ago a general besieged in the main city escaped by night over the heads of his enemies into his boats lying in the Water City. From one wall to the other an arrow was shot with a cord attached. The cord pulled a rope and the rope pulled a bolt of cloth. On this slender bridge he and his army passed.

Two thousand years of stories and legends cling around the gray walls. It has been a city of great deeds but even more has it been the home of great men who have gone elsewhere for their great deeds. Men have gone forth to trade and to war and to hold office and have come back to embellish their home estates or to be laid in the tombs which they had prepared for themselves. For these reasons and all others that make people proud it is a proud and conservative city.

By the time of this story, however, in the 1860's, the city had begun to decay. The forests which the old people, still living, remembered to have stretched over half the country had dwindled to a few trees around the villages and the grave plots. The land, left to the mercy of the summer rains, had turned its rocky side up and refused to yield. Trade had left. The harbor in the Water City, imperial protection from storms and pirates for Chinese sailing craft, was totally inadequate in size and depth for steamers, which were therefore taking shelter in the new treaty port of Chefoo, sixty miles to the east.

There was still, however, the last source of wealth and honor—the men bred and sent forth, the trader, the scholar, the official. As the seat of the Tengchou prefecture, examinations both civil and military were held in the examination halls and drill grounds of P'englai. The rows of cells were filled every other year with aspiring young scholars each of whom hoped to write the golden essay that would put him in the line of official preferment. For the great Ch'ing dynasty, though crumbling, still seemed strong to the outside world and to the nation itself. The emperor T'ung Chih was on the throne. There were two more emperors to come before the dynasty would fail and almost half a century of time. Many a young scholar still went out from the decaying old city to gain wealth and fame in other parts of the empire. From almost every family a son went to Manchuria to seek his fortune, for trade was in their bones and the rocks of the homeland were bare. A good sailboat could get there, threading between the islands, in two or three days if the weather was fair. These wanderers came home at New Year's time to give their gain to their families. If unsuccessful, the great new country swallowed them up and they were heard of no more. In most families there was more past glory than present prosperity.

In the seventh year of T'ung Chih, 1867 by our calendar, inside the North Gate of the city, the one leading to the Water City and the sea, was a large truck garden. Near this garden lived a family named Hsu who had once been rich and were now poor. Their house was on a side street which led off from the main street of the city running north and south, and its north wall was by the sandy river which flows across the city, a mere trickle to be crossed with

stepping stones most of the year—a swollen torrent in the
summer rains. The black painted, two-leaved gate in the
surrounding wall opened into a court across which was a
long low building of five rooms. This was the house. It
faced south as all Chinese houses should face, to get the
sunshine for heat in the winter and for health the year
round. The house was entered by a door into the central
one of the five rooms. This room was hall, kitchen, and
shrine in one. It was the common room. On days of worship the scroll of Heaven and Earth or that of the appro-
priate god was hung on the wall opposite the door. At New
Year's time the tablets of the ancestors were placed on a
table against this wall. Against the east and the west walls
just inside the front door were built the two stoves of brick
and stone, each with a wide-mouthed cooking basin, two or
three feet across, set in it. On ordinary occasions all the
cooking of the family was done in one of these iron basins.
Over the stove on the east wall was pasted a picture of
the kitchen god and his consort.

The room to the east of the common room was the one
in which the parents lived and which also served the family as a living room. Built into the three walls and filling
the southern half of the room, under the wide window,
was the k'ang, the mud-brick bed. It was about two and a
half feet high and contained a maze of flues carrying the
smoke from the cook stoves in the common room out a
chimney at the end of the house. The k'ang kept the family
warm on winter nights and the women warm as they sat and
worked through the winter days. It was covered with a
finely braided mat made from strips of the outer covering
of the kaoliang stalk. The bright northern sunshine falling
through the paper of the latticed windows made patterns
on the k'ang.

On either end of the k'ang was a low wooden cupboard
bench on which were piled the carefully folded quilts of the

family. In the middle of the bed was a low table around which the family sat to work or to eat and which was removed at night. There was a bureau against the east wall of the room and a tall cupboard against the wall to the north. These were of dark red lacquer and the hinges of the doors and the handles of the drawers were made of round plates of brass. In these cupboards were kept the family clothes wrapped in squares of blue cloth, for everything worn could be folded flat. On top of the bureau was a mirror flanked on either side by a vase in which was a formal arrangement of artificial flowers. In these vases also were stuck the spills for lighting the water pipe that stood on the bureau and was smoked by the father and the mother and offered to all visitors. Beyond the bureau in the east wall was a small door leading to the inner room where the older daughter of the family and the old maternal grandmother lived. It was the same size as the parents' room but part of it was used as a storeroom. Half of the k'ang was covered with boxes and rolls of stuff wrapped in matting. There was barely room for the two pallets. On the floor were tall earthenware jars of oil and flour and grain. On the walls and from the beams hung festoons of onions, bags of spices, bundles of tobacco leaves, parcels of cotton, everything in fact that a family might need.

West of the common room there were also two rooms. The son slept in the first one during warm weather. During the winter, unless there was reason to fire the other stove, he slept on his parents' k'ang. In the room beyond was stored the fuel supply of the family, great braided baskets full of pine cones and a pile of pine-tree branches. The family, though poor, was not yet poor enough to share a court with others, and had more room than they could use.

The court was small but there was space enough for laying out the mats on which the clothes were dried after a washing, and for the big earthenware water jars and the jars in which vegetables were salted down. A laborer came each day to fill the water jars from a well in the garden. Waste water was poured into a drain which passed through the wall into the street. The latrine in the southwest corner of the court was cleaned each day by a scavenger who paid for the privilege of collecting the ordure, which he sold to the man owning the fertilizer dump outside the city. A pig lived in a pen separated by a wall from the latrine.

The mother of the Hsu family had trained a vine to grow over the spirit screen which was built just inside the gate, to keep those who passed from seeing within, should the gate be left open, and to keep the spirits, who travel only in straight lines, from entering. In the summer there were many pots of flowers in the court.

There were three children in the family, and this story is about the youngest child, the second girl.

IDA PRUITT

Book One. The Family

~~~~~~

I

CHILDHOOD

1867–1870

M Y FATHER called me Little Tiger and I was my mother's youngest child. The name she called me is known to no one now alive. My sister and my brother called me Meimei, Little Sister, and the neighbors called me Hsiao Wutse, Little Five, because I was the fifth child my mother bore. Two died before I was born.

We lived in a courtyard by ourselves when I was born. We lived near the truck garden which had belonged to the family, to my father and my father's uncle. In the garden were cabbages and turnips and onions, garlic, leeks, and chives.

The garden had once been part of the property of the Temple of the Goddess of Mercy, the Kuan Yin T'ang. Ten generations ago, a Taoist priest came down from the hills, from Wei Yeh Shan, near Hsu Chia Chi, thirty li from P'englai, and became the abbot of the temple. He was our ancestor. He was a man with a square face and a strong disposition. My grandfather had the same square face and I have it also. That is why my father called me Little Tiger. Also, he said, I had a strong disposition.

Our family had been well to do at one time. We had the land our ancestor left us and my grandfather and his father before him had been among those who worked as overseers on the estates of General Ch'i. When my mother married into the family we owned the garden and the house in the Chou Wang Temple section of the city and some other small houses besides. The family had servants and plenty to eat.

My father was an only son and was spoiled by his father. His parents died when he was seven or eight. He was brought up by his uncle, his father's younger brother, who made his own four sons work in the garden but sent my father to school. The uncle said that in this way he was faithful to his dead brother. My father studied the classics for about eight years but his studies never amounted to anything. When he was grown, the uncle put him in a shop to learn business.

Money went out, the neighbors said, because my father and his cousins had too good a time, eating and playing. My father hired an actor to teach him to sing opera. This actor-teacher lived with the family and had to be paid well. He also smoked opium. Each year there was less than the year before. When my grandfather died, what was left was divided between my father and his uncle, the younger brother of his father.

My father tried to work in the garden but he had not the strength or the skill and he was ashamed. He sold the garden to one of his mother's aunts, to pay his debts, and went to Chefoo and peddled bread. He knew how to make bread, and carried it around the street in a basket. That was the year I was born. From the time I was conceived, the fortunes of the family went down. The destiny determined for me by Heaven was not a good one.

The neighbors said that my mother was not a good manager, that she could not make the money stretch so as to "get over the years" successfully. At New Year's time great loaves of bread were steamed in the iron cooking basin. If, when the lid of the cooking basin was raised, the loaves shrank, they were thrown into the fire. Sometimes she threw three or four cookings into the fire before the loaves came out round and full. This is what the neighbors said my mother used to do. I never saw it, for we had nothing to throw away when I was growing up.

My mother did not live the life she was brought up to live. A woman in childbed should have at least five hundred eggs to eat. When I was born she had only eight eggs. My mother's father, when he lived, sold oil in the streets, beating a small bronze gong, and supported the family comfortably. My mother had a round face and gentle ways. She was a carefully reared and sheltered person. How could such a person, living behind walls, know how to manage poverty?

If a dog comes to a court it is good luck. If a cat comes it is bad luck. If a wild goose lights in a court the family will have good fortune. If a tame goose flies away, the fortunes of the family will disintegrate. There was a goose in our court and it flew away, following the wild geese.

My father did not see me until I was about a year old. Then he came home for New Year's and lived again with us. We were living in the Tung Nan Ying Tse section of P'englai, in the house we had moved to when he sold the garden. All winter he sold *nien kao*, cakes made of glutenous millet. He could carry two or three hundred catties weight of cakes but he could not shout the calls to tell people he had cakes to sell, so a neighbor and he were partners. My father mixed and steamed the cakes and the neighbor shouted as they walked the streets, each with his baskets. My father was a good cook and he taught me how to cook.

My father peddled cakes for a year or two and then my uncle got him a place in a general store. Here my father sold behind the counter and he also helped in the truck garden belonging to the Chü family who owned the store. He was buyer for the store and the garden. He helped to place the produce of the garden and to water the garden in the dry season. He was part of the time in the shop and part in the garden.

The Chü family lived in a great house on the north main street and they had another in the Chang Hsin Miao, in the district of the temple of the goddess who protects little children. She can control the Dog of Heaven who bites little children and takes them away.

The eldest son, Chü Ta Shaoye, had passed the military examinations and had the rank of *hsiu tsai*. He could use the bow and arrows well. Their family and ours had been friends for many generations.

Chü Ta Shaoye used to say that after five hundred years people saw each other again—came back in similar incarnations.

Though each year our living was less than the year before we had a good life at home. My mother was kind to us. She cooked good things for us to eat and she loved us.

My father was strict but he was good to his family. He taught us manners and what was seemly for a woman to do and what was not seemly.

In the evenings after we had eaten our meal we sat around and talked. Sometimes my father's uncle came to spend the evening with us. In the winter we sat on the k'ang and sewed, my mother and my sister and I. The men smoked and talked. In the summer we sat in the courtyard.

My father told us stories about our ancestors and about the city and how people should act. He told us that the four sins were wine, women, wealth, and wrath. If anger does not hurt it makes loss at least. He told us stories of the wicked Ming dynasty eunuch, Wei Chung-hsien, who wanted to be emperor. He was a native of our city. When at last he was torn to pieces by the people in the capital, the people of our city were so angry with him that they tore his house down and dug up the very foundations. They dug away the house, thirty feet deep, so that to this day there is a deep hole near the temple, the Kung Yeh Miao, which he had built to honor himself. That hole may not be filled in. It is to be a memorial to the people always, to teach them the end of wickedness.

My father told us of the many famous men connected with our city. P'englai was founded by Lao Yang Lin of the Sui dynasty, the brother of the first emperor and the uncle of the one who so enlarged the Grand Canal that people say he built it. This he did that he might sail in the painted boats. And he built the Water City for the emperor's fleet.

There have been four great generals from our city. The Emperor gave General Ch'i Nai-ho permission to build a stone p'ailo, a memorial archway, which is still standing and this part of the city is known as the Ch'i Chia Paifang section or that of the Ch'i Family P'ailo. There was also General Sung Ch'ing whose destiny crossed that of our family in several places. But before him there was a great family named T'ung.

The T'ung family fortunes started in this way. They were a family of scholars who had no official rank. One day the old master of the house went to his study and he saw a man crouching in the corner. He knew that the man was a Master of Wind and Water, one who could divine the suitable way for houses to be laid out and find the places for tombs to be built which would bring the families fortune. He was a neighbor of theirs and not a common thief. The Master of Wind and Water was so unused to stealing that he had been caught the very first time. He had come to steal the offerings of food in front of the ancestral tablets. As the man crouched in the corner the scholar T'ung walked back and forth, back and forth, and the man had no way to escape. It grew later and later and still the scholar T'ung walked in his study. Then his grandson came to tell him that food had been prepared.

"Go," said the old scholar, "cook meat and fish and vegetables and heat some wine and bring them to me here and bring two wine cups and two pairs of chopsticks. I have a friend dining with me tonight." And the son went and did as he was told with no question. That was in the days when children obeyed their parents.

When the food was brought and laid out the scholar said to his son, "Now you may go. I will wait on myself. The dishes can be taken away in the morning." When the son was gone, he turned to the corner where the man was crouching and said, "Dinner is ready. I am sorry to have kept my guest waiting so long." Terribly ashamed, the man came out. He could not lift his head for shame. The scholar was saving the man's face and he could do no more than respond and talk also to save the faces of both.

"I was looking for something I left behind and went to sleep. I apologize for being so long in your house."

The scholar made him sit in the seat of honor and served him with his own hands. Then when the meal was over and he was about to leave, the scholar T'ung said, "Let me have your bag." All thieves have a bag in which to put what they get. Ashamed, the man brought out his bag and the scholar filled it with bread and with leftover meat and gave him also some money.

The wave of misfortune which had driven him to stealing seemed to be broken by this event and his fortunes began to mend. People came from far and near to have him find burial places for them and to seek his advice about building houses. His ventures were all followed with success and he became wealthy. All his efforts to repay the old scholar were denied.

"You owe me nothing," the old scholar said.

At last the Master of Wind and Water said, "At least let me select a burial place for you that will be advantageous for your family." And to that the old scholar consented.

A place was found which the Master of Wind and Water said would give nine generations of mandarins to the family. "But," he told the old scholar, "when you are buried it must be in such and such a position and you must tell your son not to dig the grave too deep. Two and a half feet deep only must the grave be dug. Your coffin will be two inches above the surface of the ground, but that is necessary for the right alignment with the veins in the earth."

When the old scholar was about to die he told his son all that the Master of Wind and Water had told him and his son prepared to carry out the instructions. His mother had died some years earlier and had been given temporary burial that her final resting place might be with her husband.

In the old days in P'englai the daughters of the family were allowed to follow their parents to the grave. When the coffins were being lowered into the grave the daughter saw that the tops of the coffins showed above the ground. She became very angry.

"Are we such that we put our parents above the ground?"—Paupers' graves are often shallow, so that the rains wash the earth away and the coffins are exposed.— "Can we not honor our parents enough to put them deep in the earth?" She made so much fuss, refusing to listen to any explanations, that the brother gave in and ordered that the grave be dug deeper. They dug down until they reached the solid rock.

"Dig still deeper," she ordered. So they dug and picked at the solid rock. Suddenly there was a great roar and the rock flew up. They knew then that they had dug into the vein of the earth and the earth air was escaping. Quickly they put back the rock and managed to keep one of the red pieces of earth. Eight pieces of red earth had escaped. So there was only one mandarin in the family. He it is who was honored by the Emperor with the stone men and stone horses at his grave. These can still be seen in the hills outside the east gate of the city.

The Master of Wind and Water was away in Manchuria when this happened. On his return he was told the story and went to see the grave. He shook his head.

"I did my best for your family. But now it is all useless." There was however the one mandarin.

Since then, at least in the P'englai district, women are not allowed to go with the cortege to the grave.

The greatest of all P'englai's famous men was the Sung dynasty poet, Su Tung-p'o, who was prefect for a time in the prefecture of Tengchou, of which P'englai is the seat. As his duties were not heavy he spent much time wandering around the streets of the city dressed as an ordinary citizen. One day as he was walking down the north main street of the city, during a market day, he saw a countryman from whose shoulders swung a bushel measure and a wine jug. The measure was behind and the wine jug in front. Su Tung-p'o grasped the man by the arm and said, "You are one of the eight Immortals. Tell me how to become an Immortal also."

The man replied, "I am not an Immortal."

But Su Tung-p'o insisted, "There is your name on your body. The two mouths of the two receptacles you are carrying form the ideograph of your name. It is written with two mouths. You are Lü the Immortal."

Still the man insisted, but being pressed by Su Tung-p'o at last he said, "I am not an Immortal but if you will go outside the city, outside the North Gate, and wait by the Marble Bridge, eight blind beggars will pass by. They are the eight Immortals. Beg immortality from them."

Su Tung-p'o went to the bridge outside the North Gate of the city and the eight blind beggars came. He asked to join them. The eight blind beggars paid no attention to him but went to the Temple of the Blessed Isles on the hill west of the city, to the guest house on the cliff above the sea, to the pavilion which "Shelters from the Wind." They sat there eating and drinking and Su Tung-p'o waited on them with his own hands, serving them a great feast. Then one by one they got up and walked to the open face of the pavilion and stepped out over the low parapet. Su Tung-p'o seized hold of the last one. "I want to go with you."

"That you cannot do."

"I will go anywhere with you. I will leave everything to go with you."

"Then leap out with us."

Su Tung-p'o looked down at the waves tumbling on the rocks three hundred feet below and dared not. He saw the eight blind beggars each on a lotus throne. And there was a ninth lotus throne. But when Su Tung-p'o would have leaped he found he could not, try as he would. And at last the Immortals waved him back. It was too late. He watched them, getting further and further away until they disappeared over the horizon.

From that time on Su Tung-p'o refused to leave the temple. He lived in the Temple of the Blessed Isles and died there waiting for the Immortals to come again and get him. The people of the city have placed his statue in the pavilion "Shelters from the Wind" where he looks always northward out to sea where the eight Immortals disappeared.

II

GROWING UP

1870–1881

WHEN I was three or four years old we moved to the Chou Wang Temple neighborhood, to be near the garden. We had the three northern *chien* * in the court, the ones facing south. There was a two-chien east house in which the neighbors lived. This was the first time our family had lived in a court with others. The house had a thatched roof. Before we had always lived in houses with tile roofs.

The house was convenient to the garden where my father worked part of the time. It was also convenient for my mother and my aunt to see the plays on the open stage across the street. My father was very strict and would not let them out to see the plays. My mother and my aunt took benches and stood on them so they could look out the high north windows.

I was a difficult child to manage. I liked to play too much. I played with my brother and sister and the children of the neighbors. We played on the streets and in the garden next door.

I climbed trees, and hanging by the rope from the windlass I would let myself down into the well. I would put my

* A chien is a unit of space with a constant relationship between height, width, and length—the space between the supporting pillars, the floor, and ceiling. In a large house, therefore, the chien is large and in a small house, small. The usual house in this part of the country was three or five chien. Some of the smaller side houses might be two chien. The partitions from pillar to pillar, front to back, could be put in or taken out at will. A room could be from one to five chien. In poor families such as these, a chien tended to be a room.

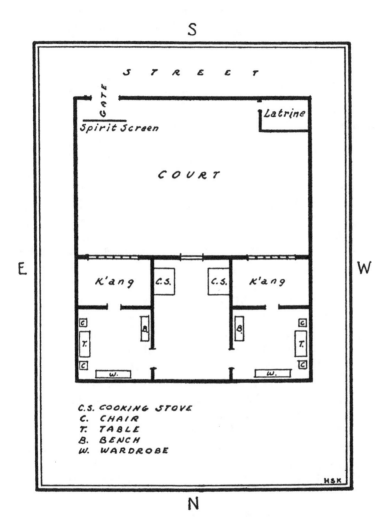

FLOOR PLAN OF A THREE-CHIEN HOUSE

toes into the cracks between the bricks that lined it. My mother did not know that I did this. She would have been frightened had she known. There was nothing that I did not dare to do. I was the baby and my parents favored me.

They did not begin to bind my feet until I was seven because I loved so much to run and play. Then I became very ill and they had to take the bindings off my feet again. I had the "heavenly blossoms" and was ill for two years and my face is very pockmarked. In my childhood everyone had the illness and few escaped some marking.

When I was nine they started to bind my feet again and they had to draw the bindings tighter than usual. My feet hurt so much that for two years I had to crawl on my hands and knees. Sometimes at night they hurt so much I could not sleep. I stuck my feet under my mother and she lay on them so they hurt less and I could sleep. But by the time I was eleven my feet did not hurt and by the time I was thirteen they were finished. The toes were turned under so that I could see them on the inner and under side of the foot. They had come up around. Two fingers could be inserted in the cleft between the front of the foot and the heel. My feet were very small indeed.

A girl's beauty and desirability were counted more by the size of her feet than by the beauty of her face. Match-makers were not asked "Is she beautiful?" but "How small are her feet?" A plain face is given by heaven but poorly bound feet are a sign of laziness.

My feet were very small indeed. Not like they are now. When I worked so hard and was on my feet all day I slept with the bandages off because my feet ached, and so they spread.

When I was eleven we moved into a house in the corner of the garden. The wall between the house and the rest of the garden was low. I was a very mischievous child. When I was naughty and my mother wanted to beat me I would run and jump over the wall and she could not catch me.

One day we wanted to go out to play, a neighbor's little girl and I. My mother said that we could go when I had finished grinding the corn. The neighbor's child said she would help me so that we would finish sooner. We ran round and round the mill, but to grind so much corn takes time. We were impatient, so while she ground I took handfuls of the corn and buried them under the refuse in the mill house, a handful here under some dust and a handful there under some donkey droppings. Then we told my mother that we were through. She came and saw that the hopper was empty. But the chickens did not give us face. They scratched here and a pile of corn showed. They scratched there and another pile showed. My mother scolded us. "You naughty, mischievous children." She started after us to beat me, but we ran and jumped over the wall and climbed into a pear tree in the garden. By this time there were several of us. My mother came to the foot of the tree and called to me but I would not come down.

"If the other children were not there I would shake the tree until you dropped and I would kill you."

I was very daring. I climbed all the trees, and one of our games was to jump over the open mouth of the well. If we had missed we should have fallen in and drowned. We were also very fond of swinging. This was especially popular at New Year's time. I said that I would go out and swing. My mother told me to wait until we had eaten, but I was too impatient.

"Then," said my mother, "I will have to call you and you will forget to come."

But I went and played with the other children. It was my turn to stand on the swing and work it up while one of the other girls sat in the seat. Some other children thought we had been swinging too long and tried to pull us off. The swing board overturned as we swung up and we fell. I fell on my face and raised a great lump on my forehead. The other girl fell on the back of her head. I went home. My mother said, "Here indeed is a new thing, that you should come home without being called."

I had my hand over my forehead and she did not see the lump. I lay down on the k'ang and went to sleep. They were all there, the whole family, and they ate the *chiaotze* * that we had for New Year's. A cousin was visiting us and my father was there. They had finished eating when I awoke. My head ached and I was hungry. I cried and said, "Mother, look at my head." She rubbed it for me, but as she rubbed she said, "Now I see why you came home without being called."

The first time I saw a foreigner I was very small, perhaps six or seven. I was so frightened that I fell to the ground and hid my face in my arms. I crouched and dared not look up until they told me he had gone. He was a big man with a beard and a big voice. His name was Deemster but they called him the Pastor. Foreigners were strange in their appearance, with clothes that looked like nothing under the heavens. But I think what frightened me most were the eyes, so far back and sunken into the face.

The man's wife used to go from house to house calling on the women. If she came to our house and my father heard of it he always became very angry and scolded my mother. My mother was gentle and liked to talk to the foreign woman. The foreign woman had a school for girls and urged my mother to send me to school. But my mother knew there was no use even to think of it. My father be-

---

* Italian ravioli and Russian *pelmeni* are both similar to and probably derived from the Chinese chiaotze, one through Marco Polo and the other through proximity.

came enraged at the very idea and would not listen. If I had been allowed to go to school how different my life would have been. I might have been somebody in the world.

When I was about eleven a Li family moved next door into a house where Ho Chü-chü, Ho the Pearl, and another prostitute had lived.

The soldiers came, as was their custom, three of them one day, and found Lao Li chopping wood in the court.

"What have you come for?" he asked the soldiers.

"We have come to call," they said, and pushed past him into the house. The man was old and could not hold them. He shouted, warning his family, and the soldiers shouted, demanding women.

Li Fu-tze, the daughter, was fifteen. She jumped over the wall into our court and so escaped. She went to the mission compound. When the missionaries first came to P'englai people would not sell or lease houses to them, so the city elders gave them the temple compound of Kuan Yin T'ang, where my ancestor was once abbot. Most of the buildings had fallen down and the priests gone away. The missionaries built their houses in the garden that had belonged to our family generations ago, and what were left of the temple buildings were repaired and used as a school for girls and a school for boys. They also built a church. Therefore the mission compound came to be known as the Kuan Yin T'ang. Li Fu-tze's mother worked as amah for Mrs. Deemster and Li Fu-tze went to the girls' school.

When the students in the boys' school heard the story they went to the Li house and beat the three soldiers and dragged them to the Kuan Yin T'ang by their queues. It was the place of the students in the boys' school to defend the pupils in the girls' school. They were school brothers and sisters for they studied under one master; in one society, the church; and the customs governing family relationships are very binding on those who study under one master and belong to one society.

Two of the soldiers got away but one they tied to a tree by his queue. Yuan Shih-k'ai, who was later President of China, was their officer. He was not a very high officer at that time. He came and saw Dr. Deemster and asked for the man the students had captured, for Dr. Deemster was as a father in the family and the responsibility was his. Also, according to custom, Yuan Shih-k'ai wanted Dr. Deemster to be the *shuo-ho-ti*, he-who-talks-harmony, the peacemaker.

Yuan Shih-k'ai's soldiers carried their comrade back to the camp on boards. But the man was so angry that he died of heat in the intestines. Therefore it became a big affair, a matter that had to be taken up by all his fellows.

One or two hundred soldiers went to the chapel on Sunday and surrounded it. But the girl students managed to slip out the side door. The soldiers went hunting for Lao Li but could not find him. They started to search all the houses. It was evening, at twilight. My mother was salting vegetables in the court and had not enough salt. She had gone to the Kao family to borrow some, but I was at home watching the gate and I saw the soldiers. I was only eleven and they did not molest me but I was frightened. I sat in the gateway and watched. The river bed was full of people. It was autumn and the river was low. The white sand could not be seen for the black of the soldiers' uniforms.

The soldiers found Lao Li at his home and beat him up and took his fur coat. He ran and jumped over the wall into our court. His ear was bleeding. He fled to Lao Yen's house and jumped the wall to Lao Sun's house and begged for his life to be saved, calling, *Chiu ming, chiu ming!* The soldiers followed him with swords and sticks.

His wife ran around begging for someone to act as

peacemaker. The soldiers beat her over the head until she was unconscious. Lao Sun, a gardener who also made straw sandals and made money gambling, a man of ability, tried to make peace. He held out his arms and tried to stop the soldiers, but they beat him also, him who had no part in the quarrel. Then Lao Li ran to Kuan Yin T'ang and Dr. Deemster came forward and made the final peace.

After that the soldiers often came to the church services.

Yuan Shih-k'ai became good friends with my uncle. I saw them often talking together.

The last time I was beaten by my mother was when I was thirteen. And this is the way in which it happened. My sister was to blame that I got the beating. She did not have a good heart and she locked me in so that I could not run away. My uncle, my mother's brother, came to see us and was to take one of us back to visit him. My sister wanted to go and I wanted to go. I said that she could not go without me and she said that she would. I said that if I could not go she should not. I held to her coat and said I would not let her go. My mother told me to behave and tried to whip me but I ran and was jumping across the wall when my sister came with soft words and said that my mother's anger was gone and that I was to go home. I went home and my sister shut the house door after me and hung the chain over the iron loop on the lintel above the house door on the outside. I was caught. I could not run and my mother beat me. She broke a broom over me. She broke a stool beating me. I screamed and said that I would not do it any more. She said, "The more you say you will not, the more I will beat you."

So I said, "I dare to do it again. I dare to do it again."

She asked me why I said that. And I said, "You will beat me if I say I dare and you beat me if I say I do not dare."

It was a great beating, and when she had finished I lay

on the k'ang. I was sore all over. When my father came home he asked about it, seeing me lying on the bed. My mother said, "She could not run away. Her sister had latched the door. So I had to beat her."

My mother was sorry that she had to beat me. My mother loved me. And after that I needed no more beating for I knew that my mother loved me and I was beginning to have the reason of a grown person. That was a great beating.

After my sister married I slept in my parents' room, for my father was home at night only every other month. One month he slept in the store where he worked and one month he slept at home. This was because there were so many clerks in the store they could not all sleep there at once.

But when my sister came home we slept together in our old room.

One night we were in our room about to sleep when I heard a stone drop as it was dislodged from the wall. I listened and heard the scrunch, scrunch of the snow as someone walked over it very carefully. Then I said to my sister, "See. There is a round hole in the window."

And she said, "Did you paper the windows freshly to-day? Are you sure there was no hole?"

And I said, "I papered the windows freshly. I am sure there was no hole. That has been made by someone with a wet finger tip."

"Put your finger through," said my sister. "I am sure you will find nothing but cold air."

My mother heard us talking and said, "Why do you children talk? Why don't you go to sleep?"

And of course by the time my father had got on his clothes and lighted the lantern the thief was long since gone. Cat thieves were common in P'englai. There were no policemen and the streets were not lighted.

When I was thirteen my parents stopped shaving the hair from around the patch of long hair left on my crown. I was no longer a little girl. My hair was allowed to grow and was gathered into a braid at the back of my head. It was braided in a wide loose plait which spread fanlike above and below the knot that held the hair at the nape of the neck. It was like a great butterfly. Girls do not wear their hair that way now. Part of the hair was separated and braided into a little plait down my back. When the little braid was gathered into the big braid I was a woman and not allowed out of the gate. So we have a saying that the girl with the full head of hair is not as free as the one with a bare head, that is, partly shaved. And at the age of thirteen I was taught to cook and sew.

My father was a very strict man. We were not allowed, my sister and I, on the street after we were thirteen. People in P'englai were that way in those days. When a family wanted to know more about a girl who had been suggested for a daughter-in-law and asked what kind of a girl she was, the neighbors would answer, "We do not know. We have never seen her." And that was praise.

We were not allowed, after we were grown, to raise our voices in talking. When there was a knock at the street door, no matter what we were talking about we had to stop. If a stranger came into the court we had to disappear into the inner room. When my father came home, even if we had been laughing and talking, we were silent the moment we heard the latch fall in the socket as the front gate was opened. We stood with our heads bowed and our hands by our sides until our father was sitting on the k'ang. Then we took off his shoes and lighted his pipe. Even my brother did not dare to say anything to my father.

My father was very strict about the way we dressed, my sister and I. He wanted us to wear plain and dignified clothes only. He would never allow us to wear fashionable

clothes. The hats we wore were bands of black satin across
our foreheads. There were silver and jade ornaments sewed
on them. They were held on by heavy cords passing under
the knots in which our hair was combed. Everyone at that
time was wearing little silver chains instead of the cords.
The ends fell below the left shoulder and little bells on them
tinkled as one walked. My sister and I very much wanted
to wear such chains. My sister said to me, "Let us put our
coppers together and buy a chain. When you are going
out you can wear it, and when I am going out I will wear
it."

Our father heard us talking and beat us. We were both
married then. We never got our chain.

It was also very fashionable to wear little black headache plasters on the temples. One day my sister came home
decorated in this way. My father was very angry. He
asked her if she was a prostitute to so decorate herself.

My sister was married when she was fifteen, and I was
married when I was fifteen. I was eight when my sister was
married.

My sister's match was considered a very suitable one.
Her husband was only three or four years older than she
and he had a trade. He was a barber. And the father-in-
law was still young enough to work also. But my sister
was a child, with the ways of a child and the heart of a
child. She had not become used to housework. She did not
know how to mix wheat bread or corn bread. She got the
batter too thick or too thin, and so her mother-in-law
would scold. She had no experience and could not plan
meals. At one meal she would cook too much and at the
next not enough. This also made her mother-in-law angry
and she would scold. Though my sister had not learned to
work she had learned to smoke. This also made her mother-
in-law angry. She would say that my sister was not good
for work but only for luxury. So there was bitterness.

Her mother-in-law forbade her to smoke. She took her pipe and broke it into many pieces. My sister made herself a pipe from a reed and smoked when there was no one around. One day her mother-in-law came suddenly into the room. My sister hid the pipe under her clothes as she sat on the k'ang. The lighted pipe set the wheat chaff under the bed matting afire, and her mother-in-law beat her. When her husband came home his mother told him the story and he also beat my sister. There was a great quarrel and her mother-in-law reviled her with many words that were too hard to bear.

She said, "In the path around the mill does one not look for the hairs of the mule?" She meant to call my sister a mule and also to say that there were no signs of a daughter-in-law where such signs should be—there was no work done. She went out of the house to find her husband, saying that she would show my sister when she came back what real anger was like. My sister went crazy.

In P'englai it is the custom for the women to stand in their gateways in the evenings to watch whatever may be passing by. When my sister went to the gate that evening she did not stop and watch as is the custom, but went out of the gate and walked south. She walked until she reached the South Gate of the city, and she walked out of the gate. She walked three li to the village of the Three Li Bridge. All the people came out to see the crazy woman. The cry went out for all to come and see the crazy woman. We lived near the North Gate of the city, but we had an aunt who lived outside the South Gate at the village of the Three Li Bridge. She too came out to see the crazy woman, and she said, "Is this not Yintze, the daughter of my sister? Come with me." And she took my sister home with her.

That very evening my brother went to my sister's mother-in-law's home to fetch my sister and bring her back to our home for a visit. When he got there she was gone and no one knew where she was. All that night he searched for her, and her husband and father-in-law searched, but they could not find her. The next day my aunt sent her son to tell us where my sister was, and we sent and fetched her home. But her mother-in-law claimed that we had hidden her and that she had left home that night for a bad purpose. So she stayed with us for six months.

And she was not right for all those six months. She had come crying and combing her hair with her fingers, so that her hair was in all directions and we could not comb it out. Then one day we found that her hair was cut, and we never knew who had cut it. Straight off it was cut, between the knot, into which a woman's hair is bound at marriage, and the head. Later we found the hair hanging on a bramble bush in the court of the Chou Wang Temple. It must have been cut off by the demon who was troubling her. All these six months she talked to herself, and at times she was stiff and still. But she got better and the fits became less frequent.

We asked friends to talk for her to her mother-in-law and husband, and at last it was arranged that they should take her back. A separate house was rented for her and her husband so that they did not live with the old people. She got on with her husband and they liked each other, but still at times she had the spells. She would cry and shout, and her arms and legs would become stiff. The demon that troubled her was not a very powerful one. It enabled her to talk but never to foretell the future.

Seeing that my sister had so much trouble with a young husband, my father and mother said that I should be married to an older man who would cherish me. When the matchmaker told of such a one and that he had no mother —she was dead—my parents thought that they had done well for me. I was to have an older husband to cherish me, but not too old, and no mother-in-law to scold and abuse me.

Our neighbor, the man who carted away the night soil, made the match for me. He was a professional matchmaker. He did not care how a marriage turned out. He had used the money. As the old people say, "A matchmaker does not live a lifetime with the people he brings together." The matchmaker hid four years of my husband's age from us, saying that the man was only ten years older than I. But he was fourteen years older. I was twelve when the match was made, and I became engaged—a childhood match. I still had my hair in a plait. I did not know anything. I was fifteen when I was married.

They told me that I was to be a bride. I had seen weddings going down the street. I had seen brides sitting on the k'angs on the wedding days when all went in to see them. To be married was to wear pretty clothes and ornaments in the hair.

I sat on the k'ang, bathed and dressed, in my red underclothes and red stockings. The music sounded and they took me off the k'ang. I sat on the chair and the matrons combed my hair for me into the matron's knot at the nape of my neck. They dressed me in my red embroidered bridal robes and the red embroidered bridal shoes and put the ornaments in my hair. An old man whose parents and wife were still alive carried me out and put me in the wedding chair that was to carry me to my new home. I knew only that I must not touch the sides of the chair as he put me in, and that I was dressed in beautiful clothes. I was a child, only fifteen by our count, and my birthday was small —just before the New Year. We count ourselves a year old when we are born and we all add a year at the New Year. I was counted two years old when I was a month old, for I was born near the end of the old year. I was a child. I had not yet passed my thirteenth birthday.

I was frightened. I was homesick.

It was the year of the broom-tailed star. I can still see it distinctly. And there were many rings around the sun that year.

III

THE WEDDING

1881

THE musicians in their green uniforms and red tasseled hats sat by the table in the court. There were those who played on bamboo reed flutes and those who played on wooden horns. At times the cymbals clashed. But during the ceremony of clothing the bride and while the groom, who had come to fetch the bride, drank in another room with the men of the bride's family, it was the flute that sounded. By the different motifs played those who passed by in the street or stopped to watch knew which part of the ceremony was in progress.

The table where the musicians sat and drank tea and played at intervals was next to the gate. It was time for the groom to take the bride home. The musicians stood and played. The wooden horns joined the flutes. The cymbals clashed. The drums boomed. The groom came out of the house door. He was clothed in hired bridal robes, patterned like those of a mandarin's full dress. Once or twice at least in a lifetime every man and woman is equal to the highest in the land. When they are married and when they are buried they are clothed in the garments of nobility.

The father and the brother and the uncle of the bride escorted the groom. They bowed him to his chair. Then the red sedan chair of the bride was brought to the gate and placed against the gateway. The gateway was too small to allow the chair to enter the court as would be done in great households. All cracks between the chair and the gate were covered with pieces of red felt held by the chair-men to make sure that no evil spirit should enter. A long note of the horn was sounded and the bride was carried out kneeling on the arms of an old man. He was a neighbor, a carpenter who was no longer working but was spending the last years of his life in pleasant social pursuits. He was also a doctor—not the kind who had many honorary boards hanging outside his walls telling in poetic allusion of his healing powers, but a homely man who knew what to tell the mothers when their children's bellies ached, and how to keep their faces from scarring when the children broke out with smallpox, and how to break a fever when the inner fires got too hot. He was also a manager for weddings and funerals, and he was peacemaker for the neighborhood. Long days he would sit squatted on his heels in the lee of a sunny wall and listen to all sides of any quarrels. He was what was known as a whole man. Destiny had been kind to him. His father and mother still ate and slept in his house and not in the small brick vault he had prepared for them deep in the steepest slope of his wheat field. His wife, his old partner, was the one with whom he had started forty years ago as a boy of sixteen. He had sons and grandsons. Therefore at wedding ceremonies he was much sought after to bring good luck to the new couples. Dressed in his ceremonial black coat he carried the red-robed bride to the chair. She knelt on his arms and her head, heavy with ornaments, drooped over his shoulder. She was a bow of red arched over a bow of black. He sat her on the broad low seat of the sedan chair.

Matrons whose husbands were alive patted the bride's garments into place as she folded her arms and legs. They dropped the red curtain before her. The gong sounded and the bearers seized the chair. They ran the poles through the loops and lifted the chair to their shoulders.

The procession started, and as both families were poor, it was not a long one.

The little procession started off. There were pairs of red lanterns on poles, red banners, and red wooden boards on which were great gold ideographs. The band followed and then came the green chair of the groom. This was followed closely by the red chair of the bride. Her brother walked beside it. He carried a piece of red felt in his hands. It was his duty to hold this between her chair and all the wells and dark corners and temples they passed. He must protect her from the hungry ghosts, the souls of those who have drowned themselves in these wells and are doomed to stay there until they can persuade others to drown themselves and release them. He must protect her from the elementals that lurk in dark corners, the weasel spirits and the fox fairies, and from the little demons in the temples who might follow her home and possess her and make her leave the path of reason and do those things which people do not do. The passers-by looked curiously at the brother, trying to gauge the bride's beauty by his features. Behind came the cart carrying the perfect couple, the whole couple, a middle-aged man and wife whose parents and children lived, who were to act for the family in giving her over to her new home.

The bearers strutted as they walked, mincing in their gait, with one arm akimbo and the other swinging, for they carried a virgin bride and she was sitting in an official chair, wearing robes, though rented, patterned after the great.

The procession filed out of the narrow side street where the elbows of the bearers almost touched the rough stone walls on either side, built from the hills on which the city stands. They came into the main street of the city paved with great blocks of granite. They turned north past the temple where the Taoist priest told fortunes and his hunch-backed wife sold sweetmeats to the neighborhood children. They went out of the city through the vaulted tunnel of the North Gate.

Outside of the city the procession veered to the east and followed the cart track along the city wall. It crossed the wheat fields and went toward the sea and a village lying low and gray on the rocks of a small promontory.

It was a village of fishermen and the groom owned one of the fishing boats. He was also a farmer. He owned twenty mu of the wheatland that lay near the village. It was the family village of the Ning clan. All in the village were of this one clan. Their names were recorded in the books in the family temple in the middle of the village. Twelve hundred years ago they had been brought by the emperor of the Sui dynasty to replace those who had been killed in the wars that had ravaged China after the breakup of the great Han dynasty. The Sui emperor had brought them from Yünnan, on the borders of Szechwan and Kwei-chou, many thousand miles, to repopulate the peninsula. There they had lived ever since on the lands the emperor had given them.

IV

MARRIAGE

1881–1887

W HEN I got to my new home and the wedding guests had left I found that there was a woman living in the house, a cousin's wife. She had lived there for many years and had borne a son to my husband. We all slept on one k'ang, the four of us. I was such a child that I told her I was glad she was there for I was frightened. Her husband had been gone many years and none knew whether he was alive or dead. She had an older son who had also gone to Manchuria. His name was Fulai, "May Fortune Come." The little boy's name was Fats'ai, "May Wealth Come." She lived with us for more than two years.

My husband's father was also with us. He tilled the family land and in the winter made baskets. When he was young he had been a servant in one of the yamen of the city.

I was but a child. We played games, the village children, Fats'ai, and I. We played knucklebones, hunting the tiger (hide and seek), kicking the shuttlecock, and coin throwing.

Everyone in the village had the same surname as my husband. All were named Ning. The old people said that when their ancestors came from Yünnan province they had each two nails on each little finger. It was a mark of the family. I have heard the old people say it was as though they each had two little fingers apiece.

They came to Shantung following Lao Yang Ling of the Sui dynasty. He was the uncle of the first emperor. A very proper man he was, they say, strong and with a good

body, a great warrior. He could wield the quarterstaff
with anyone. But he was a man of evil ways. He knew not
the difference between his mother and sisters and other
women. Also he had a troop of maidens who pulled him
around in a cart. He had them strip naked and pull him
walking backward. When they fell he roared with laughter.
When a man does not know the difference between his
mother and sisters and other women he has left the way of
mankind and returned to the way of those that walk on
four feet and know not reason.

A girl of our village was married to a man in another
village whose relationship with his mother was not a clear
one. The young wife came home and wept with her mother.
Then said the mother, "To live is difficult. To die is easy."
So the girl drank opium and died and her male relatives
carried her to her mother-in-law. The man fled but his
mother was caught. She had hid in a neighbor's house.
They beat her; they undid her trousers and stuffed her
full of hot peppers and spices. Then the neighbors begged
them to stop and not to kill her outright. And so the
brothers secured a great funeral for their sister.

The cobbler who lived in my husband's village was a
cross-eyed man. He had only one son—a silversmith, and
a good boy. The cobbler got a wife for the boy and she
was stupid. But she did the housework for the two men
well enough and she had a child, a son.

Across the wall there was a girl who was well favored
and dainty, and she liked to make herself even more beautiful. She oiled her hair and rouged her cheeks and cast
glances at the young silversmith. Her name was Huang
Chin-ling, "Yellow Golden Bell." She and the young man
became more and more warm toward each other. They had
ladders which they leaned against the wall and went back
and forth to see each other. They became so much to each

other that she wanted to join him and follow him. But there
was the wife. The boy the wife had borne was about six at
this time. The girl, Golden Bell, would not come to the
silversmith as concubine. The wife was willing that she
should come—what could she do?—but Golden Bell was
not willing.

One night the wife was drowned in the big water jar in
the court. The young man raised a great cry and the neighbors all came.

"She had another fit and drowned herself," he said. And
as is always the case in suicide he broke the jar. If one
hangs oneself the rope is put away carefully. If one jumps
into a well the well must either be filled in or be cleaned
out carefully. So he broke the jar and at the bottom of the
jar was a belt.

The family of the dead woman took the matter to law
but in spite of the evidence of the belt the magistrate dis-
missed the case. The neighbors did not want to disturb
their lives by testifying and the magistrate did not want the
trouble of a capital trial. In those days it was not as simple as it is now—when a magistrate can order a soldier
with a gun to execute anyone whenever he sees fit and that
is the end. In those days a murder trial had to pass the
district magistrate and the prefect and go to the governor.
It is of no avail to carry a family quarrel to court. The
magistrate is always partial to the living.

These were the exceptional affairs in the village. Most
of the people, about two hundred families, lived ordinary
lives and there is nothing to tell about them.

There had been four branches of the Ning family. We
belonged to the south branch. The north branch had died
out and there were only a few in the east branch. The west
branch had the largest number. Everyone in the village
was related. So we, Fats'ai and I, used to play with the

other children who were our uncles and aunts and cousins. I used to go home with my legs all bruised from the rough games we played. I was but a child.

As was the custom, I went home every month to see my mother. But because my husband smoked opium and did not bring home food, I stayed longer with my mother than was the custom. Half of every month I stayed with my husband and half of every month I went home to my mother. My brother came with our neighbor's white horse or a borrowed donkey and took me home.

When I left home to go back to my husband's village I would not let my mother see me cry. I went to the latrine and wiped my eyes. Then I waited until I had turned the corner of the street before I cried again. That was because my older sister always cried and screamed when she had to go back to her mother-in-law. And so my father would scold her.

"What can we do?" he would say. "What is done is done. What good to make such an ado?" So I was always careful not to let them see me weep. My sister's husband was good and brought them money, but her mother-in-law was cruel. I had no mother-in-law but my husband did not bring in money.

When I left my mother she always sat with her face set and her eyes wide open. She did not smile but she did not weep. She held her eyes wide open and her face firm to keep from weeping.

I know now that there is no need to be angry with my parents for my marriage. They did the best they could for me. They thought they were getting a good home for me. Now I know that one's destiny is one's destiny. It was so decided for me.

We slept on the same k'ang, the four of us, until just before Mantze was born. Then the neighbors got rid of the woman for me. They were all our relatives. They said to her, "Who are you that you should live with them?"

And so she went away. But the break had started before then. We had been playing, Fats'ai, the village children, and I. We had been playing hunt the tiger. They put Fats'ai in an empty earthenware water jar and pulled the wooden cover over. I told them not to pull the lid too far for fear he would smother. I told them to leave a crack for the air. Then I forgot him and went home. He became frightened and called, "Aunt, aunt."—His name for me was aunt.—"Aunt, aunt, come and let me out." So I went and let him out. He was having the smallpox at the time. He was covered with the blossoms. He died. I had gone home for my half month and was at home with my mother when he died and so did not know. The woman said that he had died of fright and that it was I who had frightened him to death. From that time on we quarreled. When our quarreling became too bad the neighbors sent her away. She went to live with a cobbler in another village.

Her elder son came back. He had married in Manchuria and had a family. He had saved two or three hundred dollars for his mother and brought it to her, to see her again. But she had died. We entertained him for a few days and then he went back to his wife and family and took his money with him.

Across the west wall from us lived an old uncle and aunt. He was a cousin to my husband's father. They were an old couple with no children and they were very fond of me. They had land and houses. They wove baskets of willow withes and boiled sea water for salt.

This old uncle was over seventy, a strong old man who loved his wine. He was good to me and hated my husband. The old aunt was a little old woman, over fifty.

I often went to their house and they fed me many meals when my husband brought home nothing for me to eat.

When I was about twenty the old aunt died. I nursed

her. She was ill for a month and very ill for half a month.

"I don't want Liu-Yi-tze to be my chief mourner." Liu-Yi-tze was my husband's baby name, the one his family knew him by. By rights he should have been the chief mourner as he was the nearest nephew. They asked me to be the chief mourner and carry the Heredity Jar. This is a small earthen jar into which all the members of the family, of the next generation, put food—rice, chiaotze, bread. They stuff the jar full that there may be many descendants and that there may be food for the person about to go on the long journey, also that there may be luck for those who put in the food. The child who stuffs in the most food will have the greatest fortune. The youngest son puts the round loaf of bread on the top of the jar and sticks a pair of chopsticks into it. I had to be all the children and stuff the jar, and also the youngest son and stick in the chopsticks, and the oldest son and carry the jar. Carrying the jar is the sign of the chief mourner. It is placed in the grave at the coffin head.

I was by the old aunt's side when she died. It is said that those who die alone, who die with no one beside them, will come back after transmigration as single people, people who have no descendants. The family must be there when anyone dies.

I made the little red bag which was to provide her with comforts for the journey and hung it on her buttonhole. I cut a piece of silver from an earring that she might have silver to buy what she needed, and put it in the bag with a pinch of tea and a piece of candy and a bit of salt vegetable to make her food more palatable. And, according to custom, as my old aunt died, as the breath left her body, I stuffed the little red bag into her mouth that she might have food to eat on her journey. I placed in her hand the small bundle of food which she needed to feed the dogs as she crossed the great Dog Mountain. I bound her feet together so that her body should not get up again. I did all the things for her that a son or a daughter-in-law or a daughter should do.

As soon as the breath had left her body we went to the Tu Ti Miao, the Temple of the Earth God. I pounded with my rolling pin three times on the ground to knock at the gate of Hades and pointed three times to the sky to knock at the gates of Heaven.

On the second morning all the family, male and female, went to the Cheng Huang Miao, the Temple of the City God, for by this time the Earth God had brought the spirit to this temple and we must feed it. We took a bowl of gruel and poured it in the court and we all kowtowed and wept. And on the third day all these things were done at the Temple of the Tien Chun Lao Yeh, the Master of the Hosts of Heaven. All the relatives and friends go there.

The funeral was on the fifth day. Old people should be kept at least seven days and young people at least three, but we buried her on the fifth day. All the night before we knelt around the coffin in our unbleached and unhemmed white clothes and wept, and the musicians played. This was to help the spirit start on its journey. It is natural that the spirit should linger by the body several days and find it difficult to leave and start on the unknown journey.

We put the ashes of all the paper money and clothes and the paper servants that had been burned for her into an earthen basin. As the coffin was lifted, to carry it away, the basin was thrown to the ground and broken and we all wailed.

I wore sackcloth and my head was bound with the rope of the chief mourner, and I walked in front of the coffin with the Heredity Jar in my arms.

The old uncle died a year or two later and most of the

property went to the old aunt's nephews and nieces, but the old uncle and aunt were so grateful to me that they left me a house.

It also was smoked away by my husband.

My husband was twenty-nine when I married him, and he had been an opium eater since he was nineteen. He took everything and sold it for opium. He could not help it. He took everything. I dared not wash a garment and put it out to dry without staying by to watch it. If I hid a copper coin under the matting of the k'ang he found it. The land had gradually gone. He had sold it.

I asked my husband, "Why do you smoke opium?"

"Oh," he answered, "you don't know. All the Immortal maidens of the ninth heaven come trooping to me."

He was a fisherman. Our village was on the seashore. There are two lives that a man with a family must not lead. One is to be a soldier and the other to be a fisherman. Fishermen go out with the tide. They may sleep all day and go out in the night watches. They learn to be idle and irregular. In the early morning, if the fishing has been successful, they take their catch, great or small, to the city, five li away. They wait outside the city in the dawn and go in when the gates are first opened. They sell their fish at the market and go to the counting house for their cash. The counting house is in the court of an inn. There they smoke and drink all day. What is there left to bring home? How could they escape the opium habit? And my husband was good natured and friendly. My sister's husband beat her. Mine never lifted his hand to me, but he brought me no food. Half of each month I lived at home with my mother and ate. My brother brought me grain and flour when I lived the other half in the house of my husband.

When Mantze was born my mother came to my husband's house and took care of me. I stayed in bed four days while she was with me. That is the most I have ever stayed in bed except when I had smallpox. My child was a girl.

When Mantze was two and I was big with another child I left my husband and the village. This was the first time I left him and I went on foot. It was the first time I had walked from my husband's home to my mother's. Respectable women did not walk in the streets of P'englai. We rode on horses and squares of black cloth covered our faces. But I was angry. For three days had we quarreled. He had sold everything I possessed. I had left, of the things my mother had given me at my marriage, only a pair of silver hairpins. I liked those hairpins. He wanted to sell them. I would not let him have them. We fought for three days. These three days the four people in our house had only seven small bowls of millet gruel to eat. Then he took the hairpins and sold them for a hundred coppers and smoked his opium. We had nothing to eat. Leading my child, and heavy with the other in me, I started out. I said that we would beg.

His relatives stood in their gateways and watched us pass. His uncle, the old man whose wife I had nursed and mourned, followed me down the street begging me to return. The tears ran down his face, he was so sorry for me. But I was angry and my anger was great. I went to my mother's house and they took me in. It was in my anger that I said I would beg, but I knew not how. I went back to my husband and when my child was born it was another girl.

V

MY FATHER AND MY MOTHER

1881–1887

THE year I was married my father went into business for himself. He opened a small store in P'englai to sell the things housewives need. Four men lent him twenty thousand cash each—altogether a little more than my father could earn a year as clerk in a store. They were the son of a maternal aunt who had married into the Wang family and who owned a shop where they sold silk and satin and jewelry; a man named Sung; a man named Liu who owned many sailing ships; and the son of my father's sister who had married into the Liu family. She it was that had bought our garden. She had much land. It was not much they let my father have.

My father trusted his helpers too much and the accountant was dishonest. In a little over a year the business collapsed and my father went away to Chefoo. He found work as a clerk in a shop and earned fifty thousand cash a year with a bonus at New Year's.

After he had been in Chefoo about a year he came home in the autumn and stayed ten or eleven days. He came out to our village to see me but he did not dare show himself in town or let people know he was home because if he did people asked him for money.

I did not see my father the last time he came home on a visit. I was big with my second child. My sister's child was ill at the time so she did not come home either. We never saw him again. Perhaps if we had come home and held a family council we could have kept him and not let him return to Chefoo and he could have lived a few years longer. My father died in Chefoo. My mother would not tell me what had caused his death for she was afraid that I would be brought to bed too early.

This was the way of his death. He had decided to come home for a visit. It was the second month (about March), and the weather was still cold. When he got to the Chia River he found the ferry deserted. With his bundle on his back he sat in the boat and waited. The water was not deep but it was cold, and he hesitated to go in because of his leg.

When I was six or seven one of the wells in our garden was said to be poisoned by a snake. It was decided to clean it out. My father asked the workmen to go down but they refused. He asked them again to go down but they still refused. So my father had to go down himself. He had not reached the bottom when he heard a rumble of loose stones, and looking down he saw part of a body moving in the slime. There was no head or tail. Quickly my father rang the bell for them to wind him back up. He did not touch the snake, but already he had been poisoned. Gradually his leg became numb and then swelled to the size of a water bucket. We massaged it. It became red. Then there appeared seven openings. The Chinese doctors gave him a prescription, but because we did not have enough money we did not buy the medicine. We pounded castor beans and almond seeds into a paste and made a plaster for him. This had happened in the fourth or fifth month, and not until the seventh month were the holes in his leg filled. Even when New Year's came he could not kowtow to the ancestors. His leg was stiff and stuck out straight. And sometimes after that the leg would swell and the holes would come again.

So with his bundle on his back he sat in the boat and waited for the ferryman to come. He heard a voice calling,

"Wen Chuan, Wen Chuan." That was the name by which he was known to his friends and fellow businessmen.

He looked around but could see no one. He walked back along the road he had come, and still could see no one. So he came to the river again and thought.

"There is no one to ferry me across so I will wade." He took off his shoes and stockings and rolled up his trousers. He started across the river. Again he heard the voice calling, "Wen Chuan, Wen Chuan."

He looked back and still he could see no one. He became frightened and ran as fast as he could across the river. The water was very cold.

When he got home he told my mother about it. Then he went back to Chefoo and died within a month. He had fever in the intestines. Surely it was no living person who had called him.

My mother died thirty days later.

Her last thought was for me. While she was alive I had a place of refuge. She sent food and grain to me, and flour. I was my family's baby. They always loved me and thought for me.

My mother lay there ill. Each day she was worse than the day before.

"How badly I feel. I am very ill. I am going to die. What will become of you when I die?"

And at the end when all the relatives, the aunts on my father's side and the aunts on my mother's side and my sister and my brother and our families, were all there to help my mother in passing, her last words and thoughts were for me and of what I would do without her.

It was after she left that I suffered hunger and all the other troubles.

Those who are mothers must think for their children. My mother thought for me until she died. If she had not died so young my life would not have been so hard.

Seven days and nights I nursed my mother till I could not see a foot in front of me for weariness and lack of sleep. When I fired the cook stove I propped myself against the brick base.

Sometimes her head was not clear. She got up and wandered around. I begged her to lie down, but she thought for me and told me to lie down.

She said, "If you don't lie down I won't sleep." So I lay down. Then she tried to get up, taking the little bean-oil lamp, and looked for things she had hidden.

I wept, "Take me with you when you go."

"That is in the hands of Yuan Wang." *

She got up and wandered around. She was very busy, busy, her hands moving and accomplishing nothing. But at times she knew things, and then she was anxious for me.

"My time has come," she said. "The Yuan Chun magistrate has sent for me. I must heed his summons. But what will you do? Your sister has a father-in-law who is good, who manages the family, and will care for her. Your brother is a man and can care for himself. It is for you, who have drawn such a fate, that I am anxious. What will you do?"

And then she fell to picking the bed clothes. In those days she ripped the mattress and pulled out half the wadding.

We saw that she was getting weaker. I washed her face and combed her hair. My sister washed her feet.

"Why do you arrange my hair in a different manner?" She saw the red cord in my hand. She was a middle-aged woman and bound her hair with black cord. But for the great journey her hair must be bound with red cord, and she had seen the cord in my hand, though I had tried to hide it from her.

---

* Yuan Wang, Yuan Chun, or Yuan Chun Lao-yeh is the fifth and most severe of the judges ruling the underworld of spirits and in the popular mind, the most powerful, controlling life and death.

"If it is not yet time to prepare for the journey I will bind on the old cord," I said. And she was content.

But I bound on the red cord for I saw that her end was near and she must be properly clothed for the journey. It would be unfilial to let her start unkempt and clothed in the wrong way. Then we got out the new clothes, the trousers and the coat, and dressed her. She looked at the clothes. She lifted the skirt of the coat and turned it over. She saw that the lining was red. She knew what that meant, and she said, "There are two more garments."

By rights, according to custom, there should also have been a skirt, the skirt of ceremony such as is worn at weddings, and a long top coat. When we heard her say this we wept, my brother and I. And my brother said, "My mother, if you will wait another two years before leaving us I will have all ready."

For we did not live with a wide margin. There was not much money to turn over. My father made enough to support only himself. My brother supported my mother and brought home the money which she used for me and my children. He earned enough for us to eat, but there was not much left over. He peddled candy from a basket over his arm, and he had a bamboo tube of lucky sticks which his customers shook. So we wept when our mother saw that the grave clothes were not complete.

Then we lifted her off the brick bed and placed her on the wooden bed of longevity which we had prepared for her. We could not be unfilial and let her die on the brick bed and carry a brick on her back through eternity.

My aunt—my mother's sister—my cousins, and my father's sisters were all around her when she died. Her last words were for me. Her speech was so thick that we could not hear them all. But we could hear that she was calling me by my baby name, the one she had used for me when I was small.

She called my name and told me to come to her. I went over and knew that she was trying to tell me where she had put away bits of money and hidden them, and that they were to be mine. But I could not catch where the money was hid. And then she died and we made the weeping. All the family was around, my aunts and uncle, my brother and sister.

Then I cleaned out her cupboards and drawers. Here I would find a hundred cash and there two hundred. I gathered it all together and I said, "This is mine. She left it to me. With it I will suffer want, and without it I will suffer want."

So I bought the customary white paper money and gold and silver paper money and I burned it for her use on her journey. I wept until I could not see two feet ahead of me.

Then my brother got the same illness and lay picking the bed clothes. My mother died on the eighteenth of the Fourth Moon, and he became ill on the second of the Fifth Moon. I nursed him. When his mind was not clear he called in a loud voice, "Lin the second has stolen your trousers," or, "I must ride Wang's white horse, it goes so well."

Such things he called, and frightened me. Endlessly his hands moved to mend shoes, for he had been bred to the trade of a cobbler.

I found one skilled in acupuncture. We needled him. He was young and strong. He got well. But it was forty days before he put his feet on the ground, and he was very weak. He walked only with my support.

Then he was good to me even as my mother had been good to me. But my sister was not good. She did not have a good heart. She said to him, "How long are you going to work and slave for those who are not of your name? Do you see any end to the task? If there was a son— But there is not even a son to grow up and take over the task. Are you never to get married and raise your own family?"

And so she talked to him and at last she changed his heart. One day he went away to Chefoo and did not tell me that he was going.

Our land was gone. The old man, my husband's father, now that the land was gone, could braid his baskets in town as well as in the country. What he made was barely enough to keep him alone. In town I was near my own people. We sold the house, three chien and the court, for seventy thousand cash. We leased a room in town for thirty thousand cash. We had a four-year lease on it. Houses were cheap in those days and easy to get.

I was twenty-one when my mother died and she was only fifty-three.

VI

STARVATION

1887–1888

Day after day I sat at home. Hunger gnawed. What could I do? My mother was dead. My brother had gone away. When my husband brought home food I ate it and my children ate with me. A woman could not go out of the court. If a woman went out to service the neighbors all laughed. They said, "So and so's wife has gone out to service." Or they said, "So and so's daughter has gone out to service." I did not know enough even to beg. So I sat at home and starved. I was so hungry one day that I took a brick, pounded it to bits, and ate it. It made me feel better.

How could I know what to do? We women knew nothing but to comb our hair and bind our feet and wait at home for our men. When my mother had been hungry she had sat at home and waited for my father to bring her food, so when I was hungry I waited at home for my husband to bring me food.

My husband sold everything we had.

There was a fur hat. He wanted to sell it. But I begged him not to sell it.

"Let's keep this." It was my uncle's. "Take my coat." He took the coat and sold it for grain. When he came home for food he drank only two bowls of millet gruel. I wondered why he ate so little. I looked and found that the hat was gone, and knew that he had sold it for opium. Those who take opium care not for food.

Then he said he would earn money by peddling.

"There is no capital," I said.

So he took the quilt and bought some glutenous millet and thorn dates. He brought them and told me to make *tsengtze*. All the people ate them in the autumn. He had also bought palm leaves to wrap and cook them in.

"If you don't make them well, we'll have nothing to sell." He peddled tsengtze for three days and the capital was all gone.

He and the old man went away. Not even one grain of millet did they leave in the house.

My outside uncle, Liu, a cousin uncle, had bought the old garden. He brought me a basket of melons and cucumbers that could not be sold. I had no oil to cook them with. I had no pine cones to make a fire to cook them with. We ate them, the children and I. We gnawed them raw.

It was autumn when the two men, my husband and his father, went away and left us. I had the two children; Mantze was in her fifth year and Chinya was in the third. There was nothing to eat. There was nothing in the house they had not sold.

I said to myself, "I will go into the fields and glean," for it was the Seventh Month, the month of harvests. I took my trouser girdle and tied the baby to the lattice of the window so she would not fall off the k'ang and shut the two children up in the room. This I did many days. I went into the harvest fields and gleaned all day and came home in the afternoon. I gleaned corn and beans and we had enough to eat and left over. I had a jar half full of corn and another of beans. Also I raked dry grass by the sides of the road and on the grave plots and had a small pile left over in the corner of the room, enough to cook with.

I had been gleaning all day. When I got home I found Mantze on the street playing. I asked her how she had got out. She said, "I have only just come out." I went into the room. The little girl had cried until her face was purple. She had fallen over the edge of the k'ang and was swinging by my trouser sash fastened to the lattice. She was asleep. She had cried herself to sleep.

There was no cooking basin in the house. I had to borrow a basin from the neighbors to boil the beans that I had gleaned. My husband had sold my cooking basin. In the night while I slept he had taken the cooking basin which my mother had given me and handed it over the back wall. He had sold it for opium. Those who eat opium have no face. There is no form or pattern of decency in their minds. I had to borrow dishes from which to eat. But we had enough to eat and more. The two children and I ate what I had gleaned, and what was left, a bowl of beans, I put away on the shelf.

Then he came back. He had the old man in a basket. The basket was slung from a pole which he and another man carried. The old man had cholera.

We put him on his bed in the west room.

My husband had a string of cash about two inches long —about seventy cash. I told him to take twenty cash and buy some glutenous rice. I boiled it with the beans for them to eat.

I hung the remaining cash on a nail on the wall.

I tended the old man. Those with cholera die fast, but he would not die. For two days I nursed him. He vomited and purged and I nursed him. But he would not die. His son should have been with us, but he was somewhere smoking opium. What do those who smoke opium know of family, of honor, of face?

My neighbor who lived in the same court said to me, "Now is the time when you need people"—meaning that my husband should be with me.

And I said, "Yes, now is the time I need people." But he did not come.

At night I dreamed. Two little demons came to the edge of my bed and told me that it was time for me to go. I said that I would not go. They said that I must, that Yuan Chun Lao-yeh, the ruler of the underworld, had given orders, but they had not found time before to come for me. They insisted that I go with them. They had chains which they wanted to put on my hands. I said that I must first say good-by to my brother. It seemed that the old father was squatting in front of the cooking stove, lighting his pipe or building a fire, and my husband was asleep on the k'ang and that my children wept and would not let me go. I was very disturbed. I could not leave them. I wept and the little demons left.

That was the first dream. The second was a day later. I dreamed that I was sitting on the steps of my neighbor's house. The sun was halfway down the heavens. A big demon, very tall, with red eyeballs and pockmarks and a very fierce manner, came up to me.

"It is time," he said.

"You thought them too small and would not go with them. You talked them down. But me you cannot talk down. In less than fifteen days you must go with us." I hung my head and did not answer.

There was an earthquake that summer. I could not work those days. Always I thought, "I will die in fifteen days." I told the neighbors. They said, "Do not worry. Perhaps you are dreaming in place of the grandfather."

I dreamed these dreams in the Fifth Moon. He died in the Seventh Moon.

I sat in the court under the window, making shoes. I heard the sound of a fall. I ran into the room and seized the old man in my arms, calling, "Father, Father, what is the matter?"

And he said, "There is nothing the matter. I am going to get well. Just let me get over this spell of illness. But if I should not get well my sister said that she would buy a coffin for me. She said that she was afraid to give the money to my son. She was afraid he would spend it for opium. She was afraid that if she gave him the money for a good coffin he would buy me a poor one. If she gave him the money for a poor one he would wrap me in straw matting only. But she said that she would give me the money."

I got the old man back to bed.

Our aunt was a widow living in the village of the Sungs. When General Sung became great he gave money to all in his village. Our aunt was a widow with two daughters. She lived on what General Sung gave her. When the father of my children came in I told him all that his father had said and told him to go to his aunt's house.

He left in the morning, and all day I nursed the old man. My husband left at nine in the morning. About five in the afternoon the old man began to fail. He was on the k'ang. He cried, "I want to get down. I want to get down."

I was alone with the children. We had no bed of longevity. I took the two halves of the door of the inner room out of their sockets. I put the two children to bed on one door, and with my arms around him I helped the old man down onto the other. He was a little old man and I was young and strong. I helped him off the k'ang and onto the door which I had laid across two benches. I sat there between them, with one hand comforting the children and with the other supporting the old man. For hours I sat there, but still he did not die.

It began to get dark. A neighbor's child came in asking to borrow two cash to buy oil for their lamp. I said I had money. I was proud to be able to say that I had money. I went to the wall to get the string which I had hung there. The money was gone. My old opium sot had taken it.

We counted up. Twenty-four cash would buy in those days an ounce of opium. I knew we would not see him until the opium had worn off. There had been thirty cash.

The neighbor's daughter went on to other neighbors to borrow money for oil. Money was tight that year. She also borrowed for me. Borrowing here and borrowing there she got a tiny winecup full of oil for me. I laid the wick against the side of the bowl.

I sat holding the children and the old man. Still his son, their father, did not come. The oil burned out and we sat in the dark. The old man roused himself.

"I want to get on the bed."

And I said to him, "First you want to get off and then you want to get on."

But still he called, "I want to get on the bed."

I called to the neighbors and told them that the old man wanted to get on the bed. They answered me when I called but would not come. The next day the neighbor told me that her husband would not let her come to me. He told her that cholera is catching.

The old man still called, telling me to let him get on the k'ang. I said, "You have not the strength." But he insisted. So I took hold of him under the shoulders and began to help him toward the bed. When we got to the edge of the bed he suddenly crumpled and lay half on the bed and half off. I called to him but he did not answer. I went to the neighbors and begged for oil. I begged at many doors and at last got enough to see. I went back. He was dead. He had died in my arms against the edge of the bed. I lifted my voice and wept. I made the weeping for the dead. But the neighbors did not come. I took the children into the court. I put the two halves of the inner doors back into their sockets and closed them. I shut the house doors, and with my children in my arms I sat in the court. And I was not sorry he had died.

When day was breaking he that should have been there came. As he came into the court I would not greet him. The neighbors would not greet him. We were all too angry with him.

Then he called, "Father, Father, how are you?"

None of us answered.

And he said again, "Father, Father, are you dead?"

My neighbor was so angry that she said, "No. He is not dead. He is only without breath."

Then I helped him to lay the old man out, with his head to the south, on the half of the door. We covered his face. Then the father of my children went out to beg for the coffin money. Our aunt had given him only one thousand cash, two little strings. The fates were not with us that year. She also was sick. For three days he begged and got no money. And the money the aunt had given him was gone. There was left only three hundred and twenty cash. The body lay on the door. The belly swelled and the stench was such that no one could stay in the house nor could anyone stay in the court. At last we carried him out as he was on a board covered with a mat, for we could not get the money for the coffin. With the three hundred and twenty cash we hired two men and his son was the third. They carried him out and buried him.

We buried him in the clan graveyard of the Ning clan. Our own family graveyard had been sold after we came to live in the city. A graveyard is a thing that should not be sold. But what do those who smoke opium know of loyalty or shame? The old grandfather's name was entered in the family archives, in the family temple. There was land attached to the family temple for its upkeep and that it might be well cared for. This land and the care of the temple passed from one member of the clan to another. A change was made every year. In the Second Moon and again in the Eighth Moon a great feast was held in the courts of the temple. A mat shed was built and all the clan gathered and ate a great feast and spread a feast before the tablets of the ancestors, and the living ate in their presence. We did not go. We were too poor to take a turn at the care of the lands. We had no part in the feasting. But we were also of the Ning clan. We also could be buried in the family cemetery. We buried him among his ancestors.

It was the Sixth Moon when my brother went away and he returned in the Ninth Moon. He had no clothes. He was in the garments he had worn when he went away—a white cotton coat and cotton trousers. The dirt on his coat was thicker than the coat. He had no friends in Chefoo so had not been able to get work. When I saw him I told him that he need not have left so stealthily. He was not easy in his heart because of the way he had treated me. My sister did not have a good heart and she could talk. She said it was time for him to be thinking of setting up his own home, as he was now thirty. If he must support me and my children when would he ever be through with it?

My brother stayed at home that winter and helped me as he used to. Then, in the spring, he went to Chin Chow in Manchuria to find General Sung to take service with him. We never heard from him again. He got to Manchuria when there was much fighting with the Japanese and the English and the Russians. There was also the Chinese expedition against the Mohammedans. I think he was a soldier under General Sung Ch'ing and was killed in some of that fighting.

One year after my mother died I got a stick and a bowl and started out begging. It was the spring of the year and I was twenty-two. It was no light thing for a woman to go out of her home. That is why I put up with my old opium sot so long. But now I could not live in my house and had to come out. When I begged I begged in the parts of the city where I was not known, for I was ashamed. I went with my begging stick (the little stick with which beggars beat off dogs) up my sleeve, that people should not see it.

Every day we went out begging. My husband carried the baby and I led Mantze. When we came to an open gate I would send her in, for people's hearts are moved by a child.

Then came the winter and the snow. It fell for three days and we could not go out to beg. The children's lips became parched. The neighbors gave them a bowl of gruel. I put on three pairs of shoes, they were each so broken, to cover my feet. I had no more foot bandages and my feet were spreading. I put on three pairs of broken shoes and went to the back door of the house of the people from across the Western Ocean, the missionaries.

The foreigners lived in great ugly houses they had built on the land where the Temple of Kuan Yin T'ang had stood. It was next door to where I used to live.

People told terrible stories of the foreigners and believed them. They said that they gave out medicine which made people go to them. The foreigners could so bewitch people that they would get up in the middle of the night and go to them. They captured people and sent them to the country of the dog-headed race where they sold them for their weight in silver.

One day there was a woman sitting in the market place. She sat with her feet folded under her and her hands folded in her lap. Her head hung low. She sat and did not move. She sat for a long time. At last the people said to her, "Why do you sit so still? Are you asleep?" Then they found that she was dead. There was a red medicinal plaster over each eye and one on each hand. And when the people examined her they found that her eyes had been dug out and her hands had been pierced with holes. Her heart had also been pulled out. It had been done, they said, by the foreigners.

But by this time I knew better. I knew that they were people of a kind heart. One day when I was begging and feeling sad and sour in my heart I saw an old woman begging on the street. She was crawling on her hands and knees like a four-footed animal. My heart turned over and I was at peace. At least I still had my legs to walk upon.

She had been a woman of substance with a home of her own. Her husband had died of consumption, so she sewed for mandarin families. She went with them to nine provinces. There was nothing she could not sew. She had a son. She sent him to school. She paid his bills by making cakes. She paid ten coppers at a time or five. She got a wife for him. He died also of tuberculosis. There was a grandson who was to be the support of her old age but he was of no account nor was his mother. They sold the old woman's things one at a time until all was sold. There was nothing left but the glasses she wore that she might see to sew.

"Give them to me," said the daughter-in-law.

"But what will I see to sew with?" The daughter-in-law snatched them from off the old woman's face, beat her across the back, and went away. She took her son with her and lived in the market places.

The old woman now could not earn her living. She had no money to pay the rent. She was put out of the house. She slept in cold places and her legs became bad.

This I learned years later from an old friend who lived at the Drum Tower, near the Marble Bridge. The old woman used to sleep in her doorway. My friend was good to her and gave her money and good words and urged her to move on. She was afraid that the old woman would die in her doorway and she would be responsible to the grandson who was one with no principles. He would claim that the old woman's death was due to the person in whose house she died, and there was danger of lawsuits. If it was but money to bury the old woman it would be light.

The old woman jumped over the edge of the Marble Bridge where the main street crosses the river inside the Water Gate. She wanted to die. I saw the old woman under the bridge, hunched up and suffering. The people went to see her as to a show. The foreign woman had mercy on her and took her home and cleaned her wound. She lived at the missionaries' home for many days and then she died and the missionary buried her. That was a good and a brave deed. The old woman's scalp was full of worms.

It was not until after the trouble of the big sword society, the Boxer trouble, that the words of the foreigner had any effect in China. Before that they were persecuted. When they went out to preach the people threw stones at them. If they had pitched a tent as they do now the people would have pulled it down. The people in P'englai were especially antiforeign.

I knew that the foreigners were charitable. I put on three pairs of shoes and waded through the deep snow to their back gate. Their cook gave me a bundle of broken bread, a small jar of rice, and a small jar of flour. That was the first time I met Han the cook. I went and begged from the other missionaries and they gave me grain and a warm coat for my child. I went back to my house and we ate.

VII

THE YOUNGER CHILD

1889

WHEN we had finished what they gave us we begged as before. One day as I was walking along a man called to me.

"Is not your name Ning?" I hurried along. I tucked the stick further up my sleeve. I was now in the part of the city where my people had lived. I had moved back into the home nest, but would not shame them by being known as a beggar.

"Is there not a man named Ning, called so and so?" asked the stranger. I said that I knew nothing about what he was saying. Then the man said, "I have heard of such a man bargaining to sell a child."

I was young then and had no experience. I thought, "Could he really think to sell our child?"

When I got home I asked him. He laughed and said, "They must have heard me joking one day."

I believed him. I was young and simple then. I was only twenty-two.

In the winter the rich of the city built mat sheds under which they gave out gruel to the poor. We went every day for one meal of hot gruel. We met there, for he begged in one part of the city, carrying Chinya, and I begged in another, leading Mantze.

One day when my husband handed the baby over to me as usual, saying, "Nurse her," one of the men in charge of the gruel station saw him do it.

"Is that your man?" said the man from the gruel station. I answered that he was.

"He is trying to sell the child. He tells people that her mother died last Seventh Month."

"Oh, that is the talk that he uses for begging," I said. But in my heart I wondered if it was true that he was trying to sell our child and to keep the knowledge from me.

One day, when the ground was wet with melting snow, I found that even with the three pairs of shoes my feet were not covered. The bare flesh showed through.

"You stay at home," he said, "and I will beg." He took the child in his arms as usual. "You wait at home," he said. "I will bring you food."

We waited, Mantze and I. The day passed; it got dark; and still he did not come. It was cold. I opened my clothes and took Mantze inside my garments to give her warmth, and still he did not come. We lay in the dark. We had no lights that winter; we had no money for oil. I heard the watchman beating the third watch and I knew the night was half over. Still he did not come.

Then I heard him push open the door and stumble as he crossed the threshold. He was opium sodden and uncertain in his movements. I waited for him to say as usual, "Here, take the child and nurse her." But there was no word. I heard him throwing something heavily on the bed.

"Now you have knocked the breath out of the child. Give her to me."

Still he said nothing.

"What is the matter? Give me the child." And he only grunted.

"Light the lamp and I will tell you," he said.

"It is not the custom to light lamps in this house. Do you not know me or do I not know you that we must have a light to talk by to each other? Tell me." Then he struck a match and I saw that there was no child, only a bundle, a bundle of sweet potatoes.

"I have sold her."

I jumped out of bed. I had no thought left for Mantze. I seized him by the queue. I wrapped it three times around my arm. I fought him for my child. We rolled fighting on the ground.

The neighbors came and talked to pacify us.

"If the child has not left the city and we can keep hold of this one, we will find her," they said.

So we searched. The night through we searched. We went to the south city through the Drum Tower and back to the examination halls. We walked a great circle inside the city, and always I walked with my hands on his queue. He could not get away.

We found a house. The father of the child knocked. Some men came to the door. It was the house of dealers who buy up girls and sell them to brothels in other cities. Their trade is illegal, and if they are caught they are put in prison and punished. They dared not let me make a noise. I had but to cry aloud and the neighbors would be there. So the dealer in little girls said soft words. My neighbors said, "What he says, he will do. Now that we have him we will find the child." But the child was not in that house.

"Take me to my child," I demanded. The man promised. So again we started out in the night, walking and stumbling through the streets. Then one of my neighbors who had more power to plan than the others said, "Why do you still hold on to him? He is now useless." I still had my arm twisted in my husband's queue. "Hold on to that one so he does not run away. He it is that knows where the child is."

So I let go of my husband's queue and in one jump was

beside the man and had seized him by the slack of his coat. "Why do you seize me?" he said.

"So that you will not run away and I lose my child again." My husband was gone into the night, and still we walked. We came to the entrance of a narrow street.

"You stay here," said the man, "I will go in and call them."

"No," said I. "Where you go, I go. What kind of a place is this that I cannot go with you?"

And when he said that it was a residence, I said, "A residence! If you, a man, can go, surely I, a woman can do so. If it was a bachelor's lair I still would go in to find my child." I held onto him by the slack of his coat as we went down the narrow street to a gate. He knocked and still I held to him.

The man who opened it held the two parts of the gate together with his hands to prevent anyone going in. But I ducked under his arm before he could stop me and ran into the passage. I went through the courts, calling, "Chinya, Chinya." The child heard my voice and knew me and answered, and so I found her. The woman of the house tried to hide the child behind her wide sleeves, but I pushed her aside and took the child into my arms. The man barred the door and said that I could not leave.

"Then," I said, "I will stay here. My child is in my bosom. Mother and child, we will die here together." I sat on the floor with my child in my arms.

The neighbors gathered and talked. A child, they said, could not be sold without the mother's consent. He had, they said, got another five hundred cash from them by saying that I had not at first consented. They had first paid him three thousand. He had sold my child for a mere three thousand and five hundred cash.

They tried to frighten me. They said they would sell us

both to get their money back. I was young then, and salable. But I said, "No. I have another child at home. I must go to that child also." The neighbors all began to talk and said that I had another child and that I must go home to her, and the dealers talked of their money that they must have back.

"You stay here until we go and get the money back," they said. But at last we all started out together. I was carrying the child and they came along to get their money. They lighted a lantern and let it shine under my feet.

Then a neighbor who thought more quickly than others said, "It is cold tonight and the way is long. We have walked far. Let me carry the child."

I said that I was well and strong and could carry her myself.

But again she said, "My coat is bigger than yours. I can carry the child inside and protect her from the cold." So I gave the child to her. She walked ahead, and gradually as they lighted the way for me she disappeared into the night. When we got home she was there with the child, but my old opium sot was gone. She knew that he would have spent all the money and would have been unable to pay, and that when they had found this out they would have taken him out and beaten him. So she had gone ahead and warned him and he had slipped away into the night. And she also had the child safely at home.

So that passed over.

He promised not to sell her again and I believed him.

The old people tell us that her husband is more important to a woman than her parents. A woman is with her parents only part of her life, they say, but she is with her husband forever. He also feels that he is the most important. If a wife is not good to her husband, there is retribution in heaven.

My husband would sit on the k'ang with his legs drawn

up under his chin and his head hanging. He would raise his head suddenly and peer at me from under his lids.

"Ha! Why don't you make a plan? Why don't you think of a way for us to eat?"

I would answer, "What can I do? My family have no money. I know no one."

Then, at last, he would get up and go out to beg. People urged me to leave him and follow another man, to become a thief or a prostitute. But my parents had left me a good name, though they had left me nothing else. I could not spoil that for them.

In those years it was not as it is now. There was no freedom then for women. I stayed with him.

For another year we lived, begging and eating gruel from the public kitchen.

The father of my children was good for a while, and I thought he had learned his lesson. He promised never to sell the child again and I believed him. Then one day he sold her again and I could not get her back that time.

My little daughter was four when her father sold her the second time. When he came home without her I knew what he had done. I said that I would hang myself and that I would hang Mantze, and that we, mother and child, should die together. I rolled on the ground in my agony, in my anger, and my pain. He was frightened and said that there was no need to hang myself. He took me to the family to whom he had sold her.

It was the family of an official who had two wives. The first wife had many children but the second had none. She had been a prostitute but she was a good woman. It was she who had bought my child. She came out into the court to see me and she said many words. She said, "How can you, by begging, support two children? Your man is no good, you know that. I will not treat your child as a slave girl. I will treat her as my child. Is she not better off with me than with you? If you take her back will he not sell her again? Also you may come to see her when you like."

I knew that her words were true so I went away.

He sold her for three thousand five hundred cash the first time. I do not know for how much he sold her this second time.

Many times I went to see my little daughter and I saw that they treated her well.

They left P'englai when she was seven and I did not hear from them again until my granddaughter was half grown. Then I heard that they had done well by her. They had brought her up as a daughter, and taught her to do fine embroidery and married her to a young fruit merchant. She was well treated in the family but I never saw her again.

But because he sold her, I left my husband. I took Mantze and went away. I told him that he could live his life and that I would live mine. He lived in the house I had leased but I did not go home. When the lease was up I let it go. I let him live where he would. He lived from one opium den to another. I taught my daughter Mantze to run at the sight of him and to hide. What if he sold her also? I would not live with him.

The life of the beggar is not the hardest one. There is freedom. Today perhaps there is not enough to eat, but tomorrow there will be more. There is no face to keep up. Each day is eaten what has been begged that day. The sights of the city are free for the beggars. The temple fairs with their merrymaking crowds, the candy sticks with fluttering pennants, the whirligigs spreading noise and the colors of the rainbow in the air, women dressed in gay colors, the incense burning before the shrines and piling up in the iron pots, the flames leaping high, are harvest time for the beggars. There is drama on the open-air stage. No lady can get as close to the stage as a beggar. The ladies have their dignity to maintain and must sit in a closed cart or on the edge of the throng in tea booths. No woman but a beggar woman could see the magistrate in his embroidered ceremonial robes ride to the temples to offer sacrifice at the altars of the city in the times of festival.

At noon the beggars come to the gruel kitchen where all the other beggars have gathered, and find human companionship. There is warm food, pleasantry, and the close feel of people around. There is no future but there is no worry. An old proverb says, "Two years of begging and one will not change places with the district magistrate." All this if a beggar is not sick.

But I was through with begging. For a year I had begged for my food but had lived in my own home. Now I could not live in my home and must "come out," even though women of my family had never "come out" before.

Book Two. In Service

~~~~~~

VIII

WITH THE MILITARY OFFICIALS

1889–1896

I TOOK Mantze and I went to the temple where the rich of the city gave gruel daily to the poor of the city, where the beggars beg, and those who make money by using the poor gather together. Children are bought and sold. It was there my husband sold our child. Matchmakers are there and those who want servants come there seeking. Leading my daughter by the hand I went there and heard that the household of the military official in the K'ang Shih yamen wanted a maidservant. I went to the yamen and became a servant.

Mantze was six when we went out of our home. It was on the seventeenth of the Twelfth Moon. On the twenty-third my child broke out with the smallpox. What the Heavenly Emperor sends he sends.

The master had three children with him. The eldest son was grown. There was a daughter of fifteen and a son of twelve and another daughter the age of my child, six. They had been vaccinated. My child was very sick.

I said to myself, "I am hired to work. How can I stay here and nurse my child?"

So I went to the mistress and said, "I must go home."

"What have you to go to?" she said. "To keep the child warm you must have pine branches to burn under the k'ang.

To make soup for the child you must have flour. I will speak to the master."

She was the master's second wife. She was a stepmother. The children were not her own so she could not make the decision but she knew how to think for the children of other women. They lay there, Mantze and the three children of the master, asleep in a row on the k'ang. I was called into the master's presence.

He said, "I am told that you wish to go home."

"What else can I do?"

"Let us wait and see."

"The child may get worse."

"When that happens we will consider again. Is not the time of death a settled thing? Have we not many rooms and many courts?" They did not let me leave. My child and I were given a room in the corner of a court away from the others.

The master sent out a yamen runner, who held his big red card high as he ran, to call a doctor for my child. My child was a mass of eruptions and the odor was already foul. The doctor felt her pulse and said, "There is but one thing that can cure her. She must have a carp to eat." Nothing else would bring the eyes, which had sunken, to the forward position again. The master again sent a runner out with his card. The runner went from yamen to yamen. At the yamen of the prefect they found the fish among the New Year's presents. The messenger brought home a big carp and the mistress boiled it and made the soup herself. She took Mantze into her own arms. The child stank. She poured the soup down the child's throat. The master's daughter held the hands of my child. So Mantze came through this illness.

I stayed there the better part of six years. They were very kind to me. The master would say, "Why do you not fire your k'ang?" I was too busy sewing for the children.

Suddenly one day the big girl said, "See, the Old Lord is making the fire for you himself."

He had tucked up his fur-lined silk coat and was carrying a bundle of pine branches to the opening of the k'ang which was, as is the case in the great houses, outside the window, not in the room as they are in our own small houses. He was going to make a fire for me.

I went out the door and said, "How can I let you do this?" and took the branches from him.

The sewing for the two younger children was my work, and the cooking of the grain for ten or more people. The cook was responsible for the meat and vegetable dishes. The washing also I had to do. Also I washed for the servants so they would not dislike me.

I had no clothes. In the house I wore my old things. If we went out, the mistress lent me a coat.

My child's father came to find me but the courts were many and the men at the gates kept him out. They said they did not know me, so he did not find me. He sat on his haunches and shouted, calling me, and this shamed me. But the men at the gate said that they knew of no such person and so protected me. Even so I hid in the innermost courts when I heard him calling.

When I first started working and was asked by the mistress to fetch a manservant or take a message to one of the clerks or to the master I was afraid. I was shy. I had never had to do with men.

My mistress said, "Hai, you are serving now. Are you afraid of people? When one is following a master one must not be afraid."

She quoted a proverb to me:

"A good woman is not afraid of people.
Good wine is not cloudy."

My master, Major Liu, was Second in Command of the soldiers in the Prefecture of Tengchou. As the seat of the

Prefecture and also a garrison town, P'englai had two sets of officials, civil and military. The civil officials were the Chih Fu, the Prefect; the Nieh T'ai, the Chief Judge; the Chih Hsien, the District Magistrate; the Chief and Assistant Examiners; and the Master of Rites. The military officers were the Chen T'ai, the Commandant; the K'ang Shih, the Second in Command, and the Shou Pei.

My master was a major. When Brigadier General Wang, the Chen T'ai, was away from the city my master took his place as Commanding Officer. Then we had music played at meals. The horns and cymbals announced the coming of the master and they played for the drinking of the wine and for the change of courses.

In the year there are two big occasions of sacrifice, in the Second Moon and the Eighth Moon. Each of these lasted about fifteen days. Each morning I had to get up before daybreak and make the fire to boil the water for washing the face and rinsing the mouth, so that the master could go to the services. I was never late in getting these things ready for him. If I was to call him he would tell me the evening before.

And at least two times every month, the first and the fifteenth and sometimes oftener, my master put on his official robes and went to the temple with the other officials and worshiped. He looked very grand in his embroidered robes with the mandarin squares front and back and the waves of water around the hem. There were red tassels on his hat and a peacock tail. He was of such rank that even my mistress had a peacock tail, a very small one, that she fastened to the knot of her hair when she went out on state occasions, and an official button to her hat. But my master looked most beautiful when he was dressed in full military robes to examine the candidates for military degrees or went three li outside the city to meet or escort a high official who was visiting or leaving the city. Then he wore his armor with the great wide shoulders and the embroidered front and his high helmet. He looked very grand. He could pull the bow or wield the sword better than anyone I have ever seen. His style was very good. And he was not a young man. He was now sixty-four. He was a beautiful man, big and red faced.

He had not always been an official. He had been a swineherd when a boy and then a common soldier. He could neither read nor write. He would have his steward read to him to amuse him. So I heard many tales of history and romance. He could not keep his own accounts nor could the mistress. His steward kept them for him.

The mistress was not the first wife he had had. She was exactly thirty-six years younger than he, so they both belonged to the same year of the cycle of the twelve animals which have something to do with our destinies. They were both born in the year of the rat.

The mistress was now twenty-eight, just five years older than I. She had been married to the master for five or six years, since his first wife died. People said that he had known her before he was married to her. She came from an opium house. She was a good mistress and a good mother to his children. But she had a quick temper and would revile on the slightest occasion. The roots of her life were not good but she was not bad material herself.

We were all young together and careless. It was no wonder the mistress was at times angry with us. I was only twenty-three when I went there and the cook was but nineteen. Some of the other maids were older, but we all liked to play.

The master was getting old and did not care to work. He liked best to play games of chance. It could not be called real gambling. The stakes were never more than a few small cash, too small to be on strings and use for ordinary purchases. If there were no guests in the house he played with his secretaries and the junior officials. If it was a bad day, raining or snowing, and they did not come he would call the maids and the slave girls to play with him. "Lao Ning, Lao Sung, Lao P'an, come. I must have four sides to my table."—"Lao" was the form of address for servants; they called us "Old" to give us honor.—And we would come and play with him. As long as there was no one but the family in the home we sat at table and played with him. If any from outside came we stood behind the chairs and were servants again. He would call us to come and we would call back, "We have not finished eating yet."

"Hurry," he would call.

Then we would say, "We have not washed the pots yet."

And he would say, "Leave them. Do not wash them."

Then the cook and Lao Wang, the kitchen messenger, would not be happy because that meant more work for them. But we would play.

One day my master was sitting in the court. It was a big court with flowers and trees. There were many workmen, carpenters, and masons doing repairs, the cook was cutting the vegetables, and the maids were working. My master's two daughters were in the process of having their feet bound. The mistress was even then binding them in the inner room. She was soaking their feet in warm water and wrapping them in wet bandages. The girls were crying because it hurt so much. Their crying disturbed their father, sitting resting in the garden. As he sat there resting he leaned forward and spat and reviled them, saying, "You daughters of a woman of no virtue, why do you not die?"

Though the words were addressed to the children his wife knew that they were meant for her. I was sifting flour in the side room but the window was open and I could see. Even now I can see her walking, mincing delicately, as she always did on her tiny bound feet. She came out of the house carrying the wash basin in her arms. I thought she wanted to empty it and offered to take it. But she paid no attention to me. She carried it to his presence and then she said, "So, there are women of no virtue in your house and you wish them dead."

With that she threw the basin on the ground at his feet. It landed with a great crash and broke into many pieces. The water splashed and the strips of foot-binding cloth flew in all directions. Foot-binding cloth is not for men to see.

It was a funny sight. We all wanted to laugh but dared not.

The master was so angry that his face became red even down his neck. If they had been ordinary people there would have been a fight. But because he was an official and because there were so many of us around he dared not beat her nor revile her. But his anger was too great for him to bear. He jumped up, seized his whip, and began to thrash and beat the dogs. The dogs began to run and that frightened the chickens, and the chickens frightened the geese. There was a grand uproar. There were two dogs and twenty chickens and a pair of geese. The dogs barked, the chickens squawked and cackled, the geese honked, and we all laughed long and loud. For now we could laugh without hurting the feelings of anyone.

The master and the mistress were really very good to us. We were young then and often heedless. Some people will not engage young servants because they are not as good for work as older ones, but in our household were many young servants.

One New Year we were making the sticky cake of millet. There was half a bushel of grain in the pot simmering. We had been working all day and were staying up all night to get the New Year's sweetmeats done. The cook gave up and lay down on the k'ang in the kitchen and went to sleep. I was so sleepy and tired that I put my head on the kitchen table and slept. Lao P'an was firing the stove. She leaned against the brick foundation and dozed. Every time she woke and saw that the stick of wood was burned she stuck another in. Soon every time she woke she stuck another piece of wood into the fire without looking to see what was happening.

The bedding on the kitchen k'ang caught fire. There was a great hole burned in the felt on the k'ang and in the mattress and even the quilts were scorched. The dough in the cooking basin was ruined. There was not even a small bowlful fit to eat.

The mistress scolded very bitterly. She called us a worthless lot of useless youngsters. She reviled us. The master said, "*Pa liao, pa liao.* Let be, let be."

It is difficult for youth to keep awake, and I have always been a good sleeper. I do not mind how hard I work nor how early I wake up, but I hate to stay up at night.

One evening the mistress was later than usual eating her opium. I could not go to bed until the door into the court was fastened, for I was the only one besides the master who could lift the big bolt and put it into place.

It was a pole at least six feet long which ran across the width of the double doors from the common room to the court, and it had to be put in place after everyone was in and ready for bed. The master and the mistress slept in the rooms to the east of the common room. Their three children, my child, and I slept in the inner west room. Each row of houses had two rooms on either side of the common room, which was the hall and had the only entrance to the court.

One night when the weather was very hot the young mistress, who was sewing, sitting on the k'ang where we all slept, saw that I was very tired. She was one who could stay up to all hours of the night. She said to me, "Lao Ning, lie down and go to sleep. I will wake you when they go to bed and it is time for you to put up the bolt." So I took off my coat—it was very hot weather— and lay down wearing my trousers only. My master had a good heart. When they were ready for bed he put up the bolt himself. The noise woke me and I jumped up, saying that I must go to put up the bolt. I was dazed with sleep. I jumped off the bed and took off my trousers as I always did every morning to shake out the fleas, and hanging them over my arm started out to put up the bolt. The young mistress seized me by the arm and said, "Lao Ning, where are you going in that condition? Wake up." And so she saved me from running naked into the presence of the master. We had a good laugh when I woke up enough to know what was happening.

While I was with them the eldest son was married, and I was one of the serving women who went to fetch the bride. There were four chairs, one for the groom and one for the bride, one for the matron who went for the bride, and one for the matron who came with the bride. There was a mule cart behind for the two serving women, and I was one of them.

The groom went into the bride's house wearing a broad red sash from waist to shoulder, and came out with another added, from the waist to the other shoulder. We took the bride home. She was the daughter of a man who had been a prefect in another city. His wife had beaten a slave girl to death, so he had lost his official position and come home. He was very poor, but he would not give his daughter to a commoner, and the wealthy would not ask for her. So he gave her to my master's son. Under ordinary circumstances my master, who was a military official of moderate rank, could not have got the daughter of a civil official of the rank of prefect for his son.

After the bride was led into the house by the matrons of honor and placed on the k'ang, her chair clothes were taken off and her own beautiful clothes put on her. She was seated carefully and exactly on the bed, and then all the officials came in to "make merriment in the house." Though officials and scholars, they acted like ordinary people. For an hour or two they teased the bride and made merry.

In the night those in the lower rooms, the servants' quarters, did the "listening at the house." The old people say that there must be listeners at the house on the first night. They say that if people do not listen, demons will. The listening should be done by those of the same generation, by brothers and cousins. But as there were no relatives of the groom in P'englai we did it. There were three of us women servants. We stole, as was the custom, outside the windows of the bridal room, to listen to what they might say to each other, and to peek if we could into the room. Old P'an had feet as big as a man's. She was afraid of making a noise, so she walked carefully. She lifted her feet high and put them down one at a time, feeling her way. This made me giggle. I was a great giggler. I stuffed my sleeve into my mouth to stop the giggles. But they came out in gasps and titters. We made so much noise keeping quiet that we heard nothing of what was going on inside. But the paper of the window was torn to shreds, where we had made holes through which we could not see.

This young mistress was very fond of comfort. She had a thick mattress on which she lay all day smoking opium. She had the opium habit before she came, and so had her husband, the young master. In those days everyone took opium to some extent, but the young mistress smoked more than usual. She lay and let us wait on her. She needed much waiting on. She had the best of everything.

In after years, when the old master had returned to his family home, too old to hold office, and her husband the young master had gone to the south with his general, she fell into great want. She went, like any common woman, to buy her opium on the street. She smoked her opium. She put her two sons out to service and smoked her opium. The old master heard of it and sent for her to come to the family home. I do not know what happened to her after that.

But it was a very grand wedding. It was a grand sight to see all the officials in the town in their embroidered robes, and the processions through the streets, each official with a gong beaten in front to clear the way, the horns blowing and the banners flying, and each with an official umbrella before the chairs. And their wives had the same.

There was a big fight one day in the yamen of which they said I was the cause. The young master told me to "roll away." That is an insult one cannot bear. He said that I was a rotten egg and I should roll. The old master fought for me. He asked why I was a rotten egg and should roll. They fought, the young master and the young mistress and my mistress. They fought all night. The old master did not dare to come into the inner court. He slept in one of the outer courts that night. But they talked it through. Chinese are that way. If a matter has been talked through there are no dregs left. I stayed on and their faces were not changed toward me and they treated me as before.

It was in this way that it had happened. The young master liked to be with prostitutes and the young mistress did not mind. She encouraged him. One evening he invited one of them into the inner court to swing on the swing that was there. I was in the old mistress' room. I said to her, "Come to the window. See. It is Spring Flowers swinging in the swing." And the mistress called her into the house. In the mistress' room there was a k'ang and there were chairs, but the mistress pointed toward a stool and said, "Sit there." The woman sat. Then after a decent interval the young mistress asked her to sit in one of the chairs. It was my place to serve tea but the old mistress had not told me to serve tea so I did not serve it. Then the young master himself served tea to all and to Spring Flowers. Then, as is the custom before drinking, Spring Flowers offered the tea to all in the room. She offered the tea to the old mistress and to the young mistress and to the young master. She must also have offered the tea to me, for the young master suddenly became very angry: "Such high-class maids we have. They cannot accept tea from guests." I had not seen her offering tea to me. I had not expected it so had not been looking her way. The young master was using me as a pretext for fighting with his stepmother. But it was a difficult matter for me.

What my mistress often said about me is true—I have a bad temper. I was there for four or five years and she was very good to me. I shall never forget her care of us when Mantze had the smallpox. But I have never been able to endure being scolded too many times. Once or twice I could stand, but not too many times. I have a stiff mouth, but I try to live according to what is reasonable. She was very angry one day and reviled me, and I reviled back.

I said, "You are a T'ai-t'ai, a lady, the mistress, I am a servant. Our capital cannot be compared." This made her very angry. So I quarreled with her.

I said, "Let's settle our accounts." And I asked her if she had someone for my place, for I was going.

And she said, "If you have a good place to go, go."

"If I haven't a place I'll beg." So I left.

It was in the Fifth Moon that I left. In the Eighth Moon I came back and the master saw me.

"How are you?"

"Just the same."

"Come back and I'll raise your wages. We did not give

you enough to buy clothes." So I came back and he gave me four thousand cash a year. Six thousand cash was the regular wage but I had the child.

So I stayed again, over a year. The mistress still reviled me. I still would not let her revile me.

She said, "I will send for your husband and talk to him and see if he can put any sense into you."

"The bargain was made with me and not with him," I said. She knew he was an old opium sot, so that made her even more angry. And again she said that I was hard of mouth.

"If you go you need not come back."

"If I go out of these gates I will never enter them again."

All the money I had was about four inches, about two hundred cash on a string. But I had the child and my heart was at peace. And so I went. I went to my sister, but she was poor also and could not keep me many days. I went home, but my husband was as bad as ever. He made baskets to sell when he was not smoking opium. Some days he was in and some days he was out. Some days I got work and some days I begged. What could I do?

IX

THE JAPANESE COME

1895

IT was the Ninth Moon that we quarreled, my mistress
and I. It was the twenty-third year of the Emperor
Kuang Hsu. On the twenty-third of the Twelfth Moon
I went to the Shou Pei yamen to help with the New Year's
preparations. They needed extra people for the holiday
work. I remember the date because it was the day on which,
according to custom, we burnt the kitchen god, each family
in its own home. Pasted on the wall over the cook stove he
had watched all that was done through the year. One of
my first duties was to prepare the sticky sweet to smear on
his mouth so he would be pleased and tell only good of the
family when he got to the presence of the Heavenly Grandfather and the Heavenly Judges.

The family was named Yin. There was a wife, a sec-
ondary wife, and a daughter-in-law. There were two sons,
one belonging to each wife. One of the sons had become
engaged in the capital of the province, but the family
would not send for the girl. At last her own family brought
her to P'englai in a wheelbarrow and delivered her to the
Yin family. The Yin family treated her like a maidservant. They would not marry her to their son. They told
people outside that the geomancer had found no suitable
day, no day that fitted the destinies of the young people.
The girl became pregnant. Then the marriage was quickly
performed and they hid the girl. They would not lose
face. When the baby came they would not recognize it.
They sent it away.

It was during the time I was with this family that the Japanese came. They came on the last day of the old year.

They fired the big guns from the boats which came into the harbor. I remember well the day we first heard them. There was deep snow on the ground that winter, three feet deep. Every morning I went to the yamen to help with the New Year's preparations and every evening I returned home. There was a tailor making clothes for the mistress. Outside men were not allowed in the inner court, but because it was more convenient to have him cut them under her supervision, he was in the common room of the inner court. I was working in the room and he said to me, "It is long past noon. Do you never eat in this yamen?"

I told him that like all yamen we had only two set meals a day and not three as people did in their own homes. Those above had lunches served whenever they felt hungry, and we, when we felt hungry, were allowed to help ourselves to bread. We always had enough to eat. As we were talking we saw the cook coming in at the second gate, the gate into the women's quarters. In one hand he was carrying a bowl of rice and in the other a dish of meat for the tailor. It was then we heard the great noise of the thunder of the cannon and we heard the shell go over our heads, "Ung, ung, kala, kala."

The cook dropped the food where he was and ran. The tailor did not wait to see if there was more to come. He ran, leaving his scissors and his ruler. I told the mistress that I must go home to my child, and she told me to go. Then the wet nurse said, "What about me?"

But the mistress said that she must stay. "You are nursing my son. How can you leave?"

The men ran around and shouted, "Let's saddle the horses."

The Shou Pei yamen is near the Drum Tower on the main street running from the North Gate to the South

Gate. All the people in the city seemed to be trying to reach the South Gate to get away from the gunboats in the sea at the north. Girls with tiny bound feet, young brides who had never been on the street in their lives, were walking through the deep snow and crying aloud and wailing as they walked. It was the last great market of the year, the day before the holidays. The streets were full of vendors. They emptied their baskets of their wares, thinking only of pulling their mules and donkeys out of the city and getting away. Foodstuffs of all kinds were lying in the streets but none stopped to take. All were going south and I was going north to my home inside the North Gate. I battled my way. I was knocked down. I got up and struggled on.

When I got home I found that Mantze had cried until her eyelids were twice their normal size. She had cried, "Mother doesn't come, mother doesn't come."

I took her in my arms. We would live or die together. Her father came home. He had been out trying to sell his baskets but had found the shops boarded up and had brought them home again.

I took my child and went back to the yamen. There I found that the mistress had gone for refuge to a private home in the city. The master put some grain and flour and meat and vegetables in a basket and gave them to me so that I would have food for my family over the New Year. And he gave me some money. And I went home again. As I went I saw that Mr. Burns, one of the missionaries, had a white flag flying from his roof.

Everyone said that the boats had gone away. There was no more firing. I went home and began to prepare the food for New Year's day. I made chiaotze and we ate them on New Year's eve. It was the custom in P'englai for the people to get up during the fifth watch on New Year's morning to eat chiaotze again and to welcome the New Year.

I warmed the chiaotze we had cooked the night before and ate them. Then I got out my chessmen to find, by the order in which they turned up, which fates would govern the New Year. I did this every New Year.

"Ung-ah, ung-ah, kala, kala, kala." We heard the sound again.

"It must be the guns again," I called to my neighbor across the court.

"Oh, it is New Year's day. Someone must be firing off crackers."

"Who would be so foolish as to fire off crackers at a time like this?" I said. I went to the court and saw that Han, who cooked for one of the missionary families, was on the roof of their two-story house with a telescope in his hands.

"What are you looking at?" I said.

"The boats. Three more have come."

"Quick," I said to my family and the neighbors. "Let us run to the houses under the north wall." There were a few mud houses built under the north wall of the city where I felt that the thick wall would give us some protection from the shells. So I led Mantze by the hand and we started to go.

"Come, sister," I said to the neighbor. But she had just put her chiaotze into the boiling water and begged me to wait until they were done. We managed to eat some of them but they were not good. My neighbor wailed all the way to the wall, "Only once in a year do I get such food, and now I cannot eat it."

Then, dragging Mantze by the hands, we ran across the fields covered with snow. Mantze was having her feet bound and they hurt. She cried and said that she could not go on, but we dragged her between us.

On the way we met Mr. Burns. He had a telescope in his hands and was going to the wall to look at the boats. Just then a great shell flew over our heads and he ran back to his house. They told me that with a saw and an ax he went with his family into the cellar under his house.

We went to the house under the wall. There were so many people there that we could not sit down, we were crowded in so tight. There came a shout that someone's life must be saved. An old woman had jumped into a well. Her son and daughter-in-law had run away and left her so she jumped into a well. There was a great bustle made in getting her out. Then we found that she was wet through and likely to die of the cold. So we got her dry clothes and made a fire under the k'ang, and after a while she was saved from freezing also. Then it was reported that the boats had left and we all went home again.

Our back wall had been knocked down. The actual damage in the city was not great. But no one knew that the Japanese would fire only a few shells over the city. For many it was a very terrible time. People fled in all directions over the hills in the snow and the wind. Babies were born in snow hollows. People were frozen to death.

In all, I think, there were seven or eight people killed by the shells. The Japanese did not land. They were only trying to frighten us so that Chinese troops would be sent to us in P'englai and so give them a chance to take Weihaiwei. It would have been very difficult for them to land in P'englai. The harbor is too shallow and too exposed in winter. But we did not know all this. We were frightened. The shells were coming over our heads and landing on our houses. One old woman was cut in two by a shell as she sat on her k'ang.

They all said that the Japanese would come again on the fifteenth of the First Moon. I decided to go to the village of Hsiao Tsao-tze where I stayed a few days with a cousin. She was not a near relation. The connection was five generations away, too far for me to wear mourning should there be death in her family. And too far for me to stay

long with her. I called her elder sister-in-law. After the
fifteenth I went back to my home.

But now I had no work and when the food that the master had given me was all eaten I had to beg. I was leading
Mantze on the streets to beg. What could I do? I begged
and managed to get together two hundred cash. I told my
sister I was going to Chefoo. Surely there would be more
chance to get work in Chefoo, but I did not want to go. I
took the two hundred cash and started with Mantze for
Chefoo. In those days two hundred cash would keep us for
several days. We walked all day and had not yet got out
of the city. We had wandered round and round. I did not
want to leave. I begged as I walked. I wept as I went. Weeping and begging we got to the gates of the Shou Pei yamen.
Outside each yamen are the big stones for horsemen to
get on and off their horses. I sat on one of them and told
Mantze to go in and beg.

As I sat there one of the serving women came out and saw
me. She asked me what I was doing. I was ashamed to say
that I was begging so I said that I was going to Chefoo
to find work. She asked me why I did not find work here.
And I said that it was not easy to find work with a child.
She told me to wait. She had heard that a new mandarin
had come to town and the household wanted a maid. I said
that I had heard they had one.

"No," she said, "they had one but she was afraid of the
salute guns and went away."

In the big yamen in those days three guns were fired
whenever the master went out or guests came in and at the
change of the watch. As this mandarin was one of the chief
officials of the city he had many guests coming and going.
The maid from the Shou Pei yamen told me that she would
make inquiries for me and that I should come back the next
day to the same place for tidings.

I went back to my sister and she said, "Why are you back?"

I told her the story and stayed with her another day. The next day I left Mantze with her and went back to the stone. The maid told me that they would take me but that they would not take my child. The mistress had small serving maids and was afraid that my child and they would fight. What should I do? I wanted to go but I wanted my child with me. They would not let me go home at night as I had done during my short job at the Shou Pei yamen. I said that I would go for three days and see how it worked out.

X

WITH THE MOHAMMEDANS

1895–1897

I went to my new master. There was a great household.
He was the Nieh T'ai, the chief judge, and his name
was Li. He could not read or write but he was the chief
assistant to the Chen T'ai who was the highest military
official in P'englai. My master had been a cook before
he rose to power. He had also been a soldier and had
killed a robber and been promoted. He had four wives.
Two of them he had left behind in his home near Peking.
The third and fourth were with him. There were nine
cooks, so great was the household, also a carpenter and a
tailor. Every day two hundred and more people ate in the
yamen. They were Mohammedans. So every day when the
meal was over what was left was scraped into the garbage
cistern—meat, sea delicacies, such food as my child did not
see even at New Year's time. It made my heart turn over
to see such waste.

On the third day the Third Mistress, who was in charge
of the house, sent for me.

"Do you like us?" she said.

"It is not whether I like you. It is whether you like me."

"Then will you stay?"

"It is not the work," I said. "It is my child."

"Will you stay?" My heart turned over. I wanted to
stay but I must have a place for my child. Then I thought,
"I will stay for a month and see if she will change her heart
and let my child come."

So I said, "I will stay."

Immediately her stern manner was changed and she said to the other serving women, "Quickly. Go get some clothes of the little slave girl's. Get a suit of clothes. Get some foot bindings and some shoes and let them be taken to the child. After a day or two bring her to see me. Where have you left her now?" And I told her that the child was with my sister.

After a day or two I brought the child to see the mistress. She was about nine then, and from being in the yamen had learned manners, so that my mistress was pleased with her and sent often for her. One day she would stay with my sister and one day she would stay at the yamen with me.

Then my mistress thought of a plan for my daughter so she could be with me nights at least. The highest military official in P'englai was Chang the Chen T'ai. He wore a red button and was a mandarin of the first rank. He was general over a greater part of the province. In his youth he had been very humble also. He had been a common soldier under the great General Liu, and rose rank by rank. General Liu gave him as wife one of the slave girls from his household. But when he was in P'englai neither of his wives was this slave girl. She had died and his second wife was young, younger than the concubine whom he had taken when the slave-girl wife was still alive.

His mother, the old mistress, had had two men. She had not been married to the second. He was a Shansi man and had helped to support the family in the days of their poverty. They had not married but had merely decided to live together. When Chang married a wife from the general's household she did not approve of the way in which her mother-in-law lived. So when Chang came home he gave the Shansi man several hundred taels and told him to go away. But the old woman did not agree. So the Shansi man came secretly. One day the son caught him and threatened him with a sword. So he came no more.

When they were living in P'englai the old lady was the strictest of all people for correct morals. We all called her Lao Hui T'o, "Old Turn Head." She took a husband and went back on him.

She was very hard to serve. She kept the two daughters-in-law waiting on her all the time she was awake. They had to stand in her presence. Only when she slept could they go away and rest.

She had six slave girls, for she liked to see children dressed up and playing around her. She had them wear pretty clothes and put paint on their faces, and play.

Old Mistress Chang was very hard to wait on. When she rested one maid had to lay the quilts for her and a pillow for her knees and two more maids had to lift her legs and place them on the pallet.

She loved all kinds of amusement. On her birthday there was the firing of many crackers and many entertainments. There was merriment all day and we all went and enjoyed it.

Then said my mistress to me, "Old Madame Chang is lonely and old. She likes to have children about her. She likes to watch them play. She would like your child to go there and play." Madame Chang's son the Chen T'ai and my master the Nieh T'ai were sworn brothers. They had exchanged papers. They saw each other often and there was much passing between the two yamen. It was a fine sight to see them coming and going. Each went out with horsemen in front and horsemen behind the official chair. A great gong went in front to clear the way.

They urged me to let my child go to old Mistress Chang.

"There she will have enough to eat. There she will have good clothes to wear and nothing to do but to wait on the old lady and play with her six little slave girls."

So I let my child go. But she always cried and did not want to go. Always she wanted to come home and be with me. Every day when one of the secretaries went to the Chen T'ai yamen he took her with him to see the old lady, and every day when he came back he brought her back to me.

One day when they got to the edge of the stream that runs through the city she refused to go any further. He could not make her move. She ran back and hid in the space between the big horse-mounting stones at the front gate and the wall. And the Chen T'ai came, saying, "Where is the child? My mother is asking for her."

We started in to search. At the one house they said that she had gone, and at the other that she had never come. At last we found her in the space between the stone and the wall. They took her before the mistresses, and the Fourth Mistress said, "Why did you hide?"

And Mantze answered, "I want to stay with you."

The mistresses laughed, and the Third Mistress said, "Let her stay." And everybody was happy when she said this, because the Third Mistress had power.

They were very good to us. And the Fourth Mistress taught Mantze to read and to sew.

And my mistresses were friends with my old mistress in the K'ang Shih yamen and often went to call on her. And when they went I went with them. The face of my old mistress was not strange toward me and we all laughed at my words.

The great General Sung Ch'ing came to see the master. He had come to P'englai from his home village to arrange for the marriage of his son and the daughter of General Wang. General Wang was living in Wut'ing prefecture, and General Sung had to go there to get the bride. She was thirteen and his son was fifteen. And though she was fair to look upon there was no sight in her eyes. At that

time General Sung was between sixty and seventy and
had long whiskers.

Sung Ch'ing was originally a bond servant to the Hsin
family. They held the paper of the contract. He and his,
should he have any people, were theirs. The Hsin family
were wealthy officials. But later they lost their money and
Sung Ch'ing went out to earn his way. He became a waiter
in a restaurant in Chefoo. This restaurant catered to the
officers in the Naval Academy, on the West Hill. They
were in the habit of giving late parties and inviting prostitutes to sing to them. None of the other waiters dared to
carry food to them late at night, for the road passed under the end of the old wall, and that was the abiding place
of a white snake. But Sung Ch'ing was not afraid.

One night as he was passing by the end of the wall he
saw a young woman. He thought to himself, "It must be
some young wife or daughter-in-law who has had much
abuse and is thinking of ending her life."

The rocks there are jagged and the cliff high.

"That would be a great pity. I will speak to her and
save her." So he called, "Sister, sister, where do you go
thus late at night?"

The woman shrank against the wall and said, "General,
I am not a woman. Walk by at a distance and leave me."

So he walked by and left her. But she had called him
"General" and instead of doing him harm she had let
him see the future destiny that was in store for him. He
was then over thirty, so he left the employ of the restaurant
and joined the army. He became kitchen help.

Now to see how destiny works. It was the time of the
Taiping Rebellion when the long-haired bandits swarmed
over the country. One day there came the alarm, "The
bandits are preparing to attack us."

Sung Ch'ing was cooking. He emptied the wide-mouthed
iron cooking basin. He poured out the gruel that was being

cooked, and mounting his horse he clapped the basin over the horse's cruppers. The horse, feeling the hot basin, roared and ran. He ran straight into the rebel camp. The rebels, seeing so strange a sight, became frightened and said, "What strange thing is this coming?" So they fled and were dispersed.

Sung Ch'ing became a very great general. He fought the Japanese. He became a marquis and also a General of the North. He was given the right to use the dragon and phoenix insignia, which are used customarily only by the imperial family, and to be buried like a member of the imperial family, with the use of the golden spade and silver mattock.

Years later, after he had become a great general, he went back to his old home in the village of Li Chia Wa, to see his old mistress Hsin. When asked at the gate who was calling, he said, "The Honorable General Sung." The mistress sent out word that she did not know him, so he had to go away. He then came again and sent in his name as "Sung Ch'ing," and then she received him as her bond servant. He had brought her a little packet of gold as a gift, to show his honor for her, that she might buy tea. Later he redeemed the paper of his contract but how much he paid for his release I do not know. I have never heard the old people say.

Sung Ch'ing had three wives. The wife of his youth was a plain woman. Her face was a mass of freckles. She sat on the side of the road sewing for others, and her clothes were ragged. But such is the power of money that even she became fairly good to look upon. But she died and left no children. He had taken her slave girl who had borne him a son. So now this slave girl was raised to the place of chief wife and she became haughty of spirit and difficult to live with. So he sent her to his home in P'englai to care for the land and houses and to rear his son. For himself he took another wife who went where he went. And so high was he in favor that this new wife was a favorite of the Empress Dowager herself, and was one of her ladies in waiting.

When Sung Ch'ing died this wife followed his coffin home to P'englai. And as she followed she ate nothing, for she said, "I have no children. I will follow my lord to the grave as I have followed him in life. To live on would be vain."

The wife at home besought her, "Sister, eat. Stay with me and help me rear this son." But she would not. She knew that it would be but bitterness for two women to live under one roof, and the son was not hers. Therefore, as she had no duty to the living, her duty was with her dead lord. She died a month after they came to P'englai with the cortege.

A great funeral was held and it was like an imperial funeral. There were two catafalques, his in front and hers behind.

For this, that she had followed her lord, even to the grave, a memorial arch of stone was raised to her by the side of the road from P'englai to Chefoo, that all who passed might read the inscription which showed plainly that she had done her duty to the end and was a holy woman.

The son grew up but died young, not much over thirty. He had smallpox and before he had his strength back he went in to his new concubine. And so he died of consumption in a few months.

There was a small grandson of seven. He was a very spoiled child. There was no one to deny him anything. What he wanted was given to him. What he wished to say he said. Once when a sparrow died he ordered a great coffin for the sparrow and commanded the slave girls and the maidservants to wear deep mourning and to make a great weeping of "Mother, mother," and so they buried the sparrow.

The first grave the general had prepared for himself was in the favorable currents of the earth. This was seen by his rise to power and also by the roots of trees and grass that had wrapped themselves around the coffin of his first wife. It was a good place, but still he wished to better the fortunes of his descendants. He planned his tomb in the Dragon Hill and expected that the power of the dragon would be in the fortunes of his family. But instead they went down.

It was years later when I was peddling, after Mantze was married, that Sung Ch'ing died. It was after the Empress Dowager had returned to Peking from Sian, from fleeing before the foreigners at the time of the Boxer troubles.

My master was a Mohammedan and his wives were Mohammedan also. They had many customs that were different from ours. When one of them goes into the outside world he is made unclean. When he comes back he must wash his hands and rinse his mouth to become clean again. They kept one day out of seven as a special day.

When one of their number dies they soak his body and scrape off all the hair except the eyebrows and the head hair, since these came with the person from the womb. If it is a woman with bound feet, her toes must be straightened and the feet opened out to be natural again. For each person must return to the grave as he came into the world. Then the body is wrapped in white cloth. Men care for the men, and women for the women. The Koran is read and incense is burned. There was no death in the family while I was with them, but they told me these things.

Every spring they fasted for forty days. They had a big meal in the morning before the sun rose, then ate nothing and drank nothing until after the sun set. They ate no pork, only mutton, and the sheep was killed by their own chief cook. He wore a tall hat and said some words—I suppose it was a charm—over the knife, and then plunged it into the sheep.

One day I was sitting with the mistresses when Autumn Chrysanthemum, the slave girl of the Third Mistress, came running in. The slave girl belonging to the Fourth Mistress was called Spring Flower. Autumn Chrysanthemum said, "The oil boils in the pot."

The mistress said, "Has he entered the oil?" And the child said that he had.

I had heard stories of the barbarous doings of those of foreign religions, and I had seen some strange things. I thought, "Do they really put the old man into the boiling oil?"

So I slipped out of the room and went back to the kitchen quarters. There I saw the old man, the cook, with a funny tall black hat on his head and a broad short-handled spoon in his hand, jumping around a great pot of boiling oil. He was frying cakes in deep fat. They use these cakes for ceremonies and for presents to each other. They will not let those of us outside the religion eat of them unless they first break the cakes. He was making these cakes in their special way and the mistress had used the words, "Has he entered the oil?" meaning, "Has he put the cakes into the oil?" I had a good laugh at myself.

Life was very easy with the Li family. My work was not hard and we had plenty to eat. If I said, as I often did, that my destiny was a poor one, the Third Mistress would rebuke me.

"Have you not come to live with us? Do not the rich rely on heaven and the poor rely on the rich?"

The master had gone to the capital of the province to transact some business with the governor. He was gone for a month. He took his official seal with him. As we all know, the official seal is a powerful thing. It can press down and keep in place that which should be kept in place. When the seal is away many elements are free to work in ways that they should not.

One day the mistresses went for a walk in the compound. Through the courts they went, down the archers' lane to the south, to the temple of Kuan Kung, the God of War, he that was not born of woman and had never passed through the red gate.

Now the customs of the house were very strict. No man was allowed to enter beyond the second gate. Always when one of the mistresses wanted anything she would tell one of us and we would go to the second gate and call the cook or the boy or tell the steward what was wanted.

Now the Third Mistress said, "The tailor is an old man. Let us have him in here to cut out my new clothes by my own instructions."

The tailor was called. We put two square tables together and laid a felt on top. He sat there cutting the cloth according to the instructions of the Third Mistress. He was a tailor who lived in the yamen and worked always for the mistresses. The Fourth Mistress went into an inner room to take a bath. They were Mohammedans and took many ceremonial baths.

Suddenly there came from the inner room a sound that was not human, a gasp and a loud cry. I was sitting watching the tailor. We rushed to the door but it was locked. We called, but there was no answer, only the loud inhuman noises. I was young and strong in those days, so I lifted the door from its socket and we rushed in. The men had come by now, the old steward and another old man, a nephew of the house. There was the Fourth Mistress lying back against the wall on the k'ang. Fortunately she had on a pair of trousers. Otherwise she was bare. Even her

feet were not covered. The old steward put his hand on her
mouth and said, "What is the matter?" He was an old
servant and dared to do so.

She called in a loud voice, "I am Kuan Kung."

"What do you want?" we all called together.

"I want a sword," she called in a loud voice.

"All right, all right," we answered, "we will get it for
you." But still she called and cried in that strange voice.

So we asked again what she wanted, and she said, "A
cannon." There was also a cannon in the lane of the archers, so we promised to take that also to her temple, the
Temple of Kuan Kung. But still the god would not leave
her.

"I want a flowered cannon." That also they promised to
her, thinking that the god in her wanted one of those cannon cast with dragons on it. But she became very angry
and we knew that we had not heard aright. It was an embroidered robe she wanted, or rather the god wanted. That
too was promised to her, and a new set of hangings for the
temple.

Still she would not stop calling. And the old steward
asked again, "Why do you call so?"

And she answered, "The Third Mistress spends all her
time reading the *Three Kingdoms*,* and the heroes say that
she is too familiar with them."

We all knew that the two mistresses spent much of their
time reading the romance of the *Three Kingdoms*, about
Kuan Kung when he was a man, and about his master and

* *Three Kingdoms* is a historical romance of the period of disintegra-
tion at the end of the Han dynasty and the interregnum before the next
dynasty, approximately the first half of the third century A.D. The
stories were handed down orally and collected, according to some au-
thorities, into book form in the late fourteenth century by Lo Kuan-chung.
It was translated by C. H. Brewitt-Taylor with the title *San Kuo or
the Romance of the Three Kingdoms* and published by Kelley and Walsh,
Shanghai.

friend Liu Pei, the heir of the Han dynasty. So we all hunted for the books. The god, we thought, had come for his books. We found several sets and took them away. She still called, so we looked further, and in the wall table in the end drawer another set was found. We took those also. Still she called.

At last the old nephew brought in a shaman, a man who could talk to the spirits and the demons. He burned incense to the god inside the Fourth Mistress, and he burned paper money. At last he was able to lead the god step by step out of the house, across the courts, back down the lane of the archers, back to his own temple. The Fourth Mistress became quiet, but still she had spells of calling.

When there was peace again, we were sitting one day in the Third Mistress' room. When there were no guests the servants and the mistresses sat together. The two mistresses were sitting on the k'ang. The Fourth Mistress was reading and the Third Mistress was warming her hands on a small hand stove. There was a charcoal brazier in the room but there were no coal stoves, as now, so the Third Mistress was warming her hands on the small hand stove. I was sitting on a bench by the k'ang. I was sewing, making an apron for the daughter of the family who was at home with her mother, the First Mistress. It was to be sent to her. My head began to sag.

"What is the matter, Lao Ning? Are you sleepy?" But I said that I was all right. Then I began to sway.

So the Fourth Mistress said, "You do not look well. You had better go to your room and lie down for a while."

But when I got up to go I sagged over and sank to the ground. In falling I slipped across the bed on which the mistresses were sitting. The last thing I remember was hearing the Third Mistress say, "So you think you will lie on my bed, do you?" The rest they have told me.

The Third Mistress was so frightened she jumped off

the bed in her stocking feet and ran around the room. "What is this that you all should frighten me so? First the Fourth Mistress and now you."

The children, the little slave girls and my daughter, began to cry, "Mother, mother, are you dead?" and, "Auntie, auntie, are you dead?" The little slave girls called me auntie. With all the noise the menservants came in. The old nephew lifted me to a sitting position and hung my head between my knees and called my name. They said that after a long time he managed to call me back.

I don't remember anything that happened when I was in the land of the dead. But coming back there was a roaring and I felt very uncomfortable indeed. Then I vomited and immediately was all right. The cook went out to get some ashes to sweep up the vomit but I took the broom from him. I felt well and full of strength and able to sweep myself. They sent me off to bed and I was quite myself the next day.

The Third Mistress was very angry with me. She said that I had given her a great fright.

Three times in my life I have died. Never did I see anything when I was in the other world, so I do not know whether I went to heaven or to hell. There was a rushing in my ears, a roar, and then another roar, and everything was gray. The first time I died was when I was going to the gruel station. Mantze had slipped into the shed but I had not yet succeeded in pushing in. Suddenly I felt queer. There were tufts of grass growing in the wall. I seized them but there was no hold in them and I sank in a heap to the ground. I did not know what happened but they told me about it afterward. There was a great commotion.

"A person has died; a person has died."

And they said, "Is it not so-and-so?" and "Is it so-and-so?"

Someone called my daughter out of the shed. And she wept and called, "Mother. Mother is dead."

Someone belonging to the gruel station raised me and bent over and called me, calling my spirit to return, so that after a while I came alive again and went in to get my bowl of gruel. There was no ill effect; I felt the same as before.

The second time I died was this time when I was with the family of the Nieh T'ai.

My master was a very tall man and well grown. His shoulders were broad. He had a big nose and his eyes were fierce. We were all afraid of him. He dyed his eyebrows and his moustache to keep them black. He was even more fierce when we saw him at night with the dye paste on his face. We were so much afraid of him that when he gave orders we stood meekly and stuttered. The Third Mistress would become very angry with us and say, "Are you all stupid stutterers? Can none of you talk straight?" But when the master looked at us with his big fierce eyes we were afraid of him and afraid that we would say something wrong and make him angry.

The Third Mistress had been a slave girl but had borne the master two sons. That gave her a special position. But the two sons were at the old home with the first wife. According to custom they belonged to the first wife and counted as hers. She was bringing them up and educating them.

The Fourth Mistress had been taken from a house with a public gate. She had been a prostitute and so had no children. It was her duty to keep the master's official robes and insignia and to dress him when he went out. When an official dressed in his robes there was much to do for him. The folds of the robes must be arranged to fall correctly. The buttons and sashes must be fastened and some of them were fastened behind. The mandarin beads must be hung correctly around his neck. When the Fourth Mistress was out we did this for him.

There was marked jealousy between the Third Mistress and the Fourth Mistress. If the master went to the Third Mistress' room the Fourth Mistress did not like it. If he went to the Fourth Mistress' room the Third Mistress did not like it. But at other times they were good enough friends.

When the Third Mistress and the Fourth Mistress quarreled it was always over the master. They had rooms on either side of the common room, the Third Mistress on the east and the Fourth Mistress on the west. For ten days— or was it five?—he lived in one room and for ten days in the other. After a night or two the one with whom he was not always became angry. She would see me bringing in the urinal for the night. "Take it to that room. It does not belong here."

When they were unhappy they even used me as a pretext for quarreling. Third Mistress would say, "I hired you— you must listen to me. When she calls do not move."

And I answered, "That is not according to what is right. When you call I come. When I am idle and she calls, I should go there also." The face of the Third Mistress became red. She had been a slave girl and I had been brought up in a family.

The two women quarreled and this one told the master her tale and that one told him her tale. One day the Fourth Mistress was dressing the master. The mistresses had been quarreling. He said to the Fourth Mistress, "Now apologize."

The Fourth Mistress stamped her foot and said that she would not. She went into her room and slammed the door.

The Third Mistress went into her room and slammed the door.

The master sat at the table in the common room. He sat a while and then he said, "Lao Ning, give the order that I am leaving. I have calls to make."

So I went to the second gate and called the order that the master was leaving. There was the matter of the cannon to be fired when the master went out on official calls, and the chair to be brought and the horsemen and their horses.

When the master had gone I went to the wife of his chief secretary who was also a Mohammedan and I got her to come to make peace between the two mistresses. All day she stayed there and we talked. All day we talked, and at last peace was made between them.

When the master came home, before he came into the court, when I opened the second gate for him, he asked, "Have they made peace?" And I told him that the wife of the secretary and I had made peace for them.

I brought him a cup of tea and he said, "Whoever had two such things for wives? Do not tell this matter outside our court."

He was a man of principle. He would say, "Excess is sin. Drink but do not get drunk. Copulate but not to satiety. Only those who smoke opium too much cannot control themselves."

He was fond, too, of a good time. When there were no guests he would have the second gate shut and call us all in. "Come," he would say, "let us sing." Then we would all come, menservants and maidservants and the family, and we would all sing and make music.

But his leg was bad. It had been hurt in fighting. He had a bullet wound in his leg.

My master was promoted and they had to go to another city. Also his legs were bad and he was thinking of retiring. His knees ached. They wanted me to go with them but I said that I could not. I could not go that far from home, for they lived in another province. So my mistress introduced me to all her friends and asked them all to think for me and to find me a position because I had no family to think for me and help me. My mistress was a good woman. She took the responsibility that a mistress should take for those that serve her, to plan for them and make sure that they would eat.

Then my mistress thought of the old peddler woman, Liu Ma, and sent for her and told her to be my sworn mother, that I might have someone with whom to advise and to whom I could go for a meal in time of hunger. Liu Ma acknowledged me as her sworn daughter in the presence of my mistress and my mistress told her to find work for me as she went from yamen to yamen, peddling her wares to the wives of the officials.

My master's mother had been married twice, both times to men of the name of Li, and she had five sons all of whom were high officials. Two of them were of the highest rank and wore red buttons. One of these was my master. The two who wore blue buttons were in Chinanfu with the governor. The third son was of the white-button rank and lived in Chefoo. When the family left P'englai he came to see them off and told me that if ever I needed work I was to come to him in Chefoo and he would give me work. He had a theater in Chefoo and made enough and more.

When I packed my things and took my formal leave they were all sorry to see me go. They wept when they parted from me. As they were getting into their carts to go away, the Third Mistress said, "Lao Ning, you are young and there is time for you to change. You are a good woman. You work well and your heart is good. You have only one fault. You are too hot tempered. You cannot bear to hear any words against you. Are others not people also? You must learn to see also with their eyes and to control your tongue."

Then my mistress went away and I went to the house of the Yang family. He was a military official and a Mohammedan, and my mistress had asked them to take care of me. I stayed there perhaps ten or twenty days. Mistress Yang said, "There is food for you in this house and for your child, but I cannot give you money." She already had two maids. There was nothing for me to do, and when I looked for work I saw that it was theirs and I would spoil their places for them if I worked.

Of extra sewing there was little, so I became restless. I said that I would go to Chefoo to the Third Master. But they all urged me to stay in P'englai, so I went to my sworn mother and she found a position for me in the family of the assistant prefect and I was to take the child with me.

So I left her for the time with Mistress Yang and I went to the assistant prefect's family to see.

The assistant prefect was old, a little shriveled man with a little sparse beard, and he mumbled. His wife also was old and she smoked opium. They were not people who cared for appearances. All they had went for opium. The young master was a rabbit. He minced as he walked and swayed like a woman. He did not care for his wife. He spent his time with actors and with female impersonators. The young mistress went around in clothes that were poorer and dirtier than mine. She wore a little short wadded jacket that did not meet the trousers behind and showed a strip of her back. What had she that could make her care how she looked?

I got there in the afternoon. There were six maids. We sat down at the table. All we had to eat was third-grade rice and cabbage soup. There was no order. Each grabbed for herself and I did not get enough to eat.

Then I was shown to the big room where we were all to sleep, six on one bed. I spread my quilt on the bed with the others and lay down to sleep. They rolled and tossed, and with each rolling and tossing the bed shook. Suddenly there was a bite on my neck. I grabbed and caught a big louse. The lice bit until morning. I got up and started to work. Soon it was noon but still there was no food and I was very hungry. There were but two meals a day and the first was served when the old mistress got up. And she was still sleeping her opium sleep. The maids had each hidden a bowl of rice in the room to eat when they were hungry, but I had had no experience. The old master had got up but the mistress had not.

I went to the young mistress and said that I had left something at the home of my sworn mother and that I must go for it. She said for me to wait until I had had breakfast, but I said that I would eat at the house of my sworn mother. She said for me to wait and see the old mistress. But since she was an opium smoker there was no telling when she would wake. Then the young mistress took me to the master.

"You wish to leave?"

"I have left something very important at the home of my sworn mother. I must go for it." How could a man ask a woman what of importance she had left behind? So he let me go.

I went to my sworn mother and I said, "I cannot live in that place. Till now I have had nothing to eat. I am used to three meals a day. I am not afraid of hard work but I am afraid of hunger, and how could the child stand it? She could not wait to eat until this time of the day. Where we were before, we ate when hungry." My sworn mother was eating her meal and asked me to eat with her. I ate and then she went out to find me another job. But I said that I would go to Chefoo to the Third Master.

I had the mule litter hired and was packing to go when my sworn mother came to say that she had found a job for me with the assistant to the district magistrate. Mistress Yang and all my friends urged me to stay. So I went to the house of Ch'ien Lao-yeh, the assistant to the district magistrate.

They also had but two meals a day. The food was contracted for by the cook. He supplied only two meals, and if we were not there when it was time to eat we got nothing. The food was put away. And I was asked to empty the night pail, for they were southerners. I had never emptied a night pail and I did not like to do it. The other families where I had worked were all northerners. They used the latrine in the corner of the court or back of the house, as all we northerners do. My girl was growing. How could she live on two meals a day with no chance to eat on the side? So I went back to my sworn mother and I said to her that I was going to Chefoo to the Third Master. Surely in his household or in those of his friends there would be work for me. But all urged me to stay. Seeing that my mind was made up, Mistress Yang told her son to make arrangements for me to go by boat.

I made the rounds of my old mistresses to tell them I was going. They each told me to stay. They said, "Your friends and relatives are all here. In Chefoo are only people you do not know. How will you be sure that you will fare well with them? Stay with us."

When I got to Mistress Liu of the K'ang Shih yamen, my first mistress, she said, "You were always stubborn, Lao Ning. Here, drink the parting cup of wine with me, but leave the child behind. I will care for her."

My things were wrapped and ready to start when I remembered that I had left a pair of Mantze's shoes in the assistant district magistrate's yamen. I went to get them. When I entered the gate they all surrounded me and said, "Where have you been? We did not know where the house of Mandarin Yang was and so could not find you. We have hunted for you everywhere. Our mistress sent us out to find you."

When I went in to see the mistress she said to me, "Where have you been? The maid that you left in your place has gone, and I want you to come back to us. And also I have made a new arrangement with the cook. He is too hard on people and clears off the table too quickly. He is now to cook the meats and the vegetables only. I have told the small boy to cook the rice. And the crisp crusts of rice he is to save for the child to eat when she wishes, and he may fry them in fat for her."

I was stubborn, and I said that I would consult my sworn mother. But she also urged me to stay.

"The work there is light," she said. "You have only to comb the hair of the mistress and that of her two daughters and to wait on table. Now, can you be sure of so good a place in Chefoo? Is not the child old enough to carry out the night pail for you?"

And so I stayed, and I stayed there almost three years.

XI

WITH THE CIVIL OFFICIALS

1897–1899

M Y NEW master Ch'ien Lao-yeh had passed his examinations and was qualified to be a district magistrate himself. He had the rank, but as yet had never been given an official seal of his own. He was called a "Waiting to Re-place District Magistrate." Meantime he worked as assistant to the district magistrate of P'englai. He worked up most of the lawsuits. He had no salary but got his share of what is paid by those who go to law. His father had been a prefect. They came from an old family of famous lawyers. No court in China was considered complete without a Ch'ien of Hsiao Hsing.

The clan family had not divided the property for seventeen generations. There were over two hundred rooms in the house in Hsiao Hsing. When the family went to meals there were between two and three hundred people fed at every meal. A gong was beaten and all went. The house was open to any member of the family at any time, and he could stay as long as he wished. When a girl of the family was married she was given ten dollars, and when a man was married he was given twenty dollars. This was done no matter what the private wealth of the person or how poor he was.

The master himself was a man of rectitude and breeding. For a long time he did not know that my face was covered with pockmarks. He had never looked at me. When he walked it was with head lowered. He looked neither to the right nor to the left. One day when I had been there a year and a half he happened to look up as I was setting the tea in front of him. I saw him start. He waited until I was out of the room. He did not have the face to say it while I was there. He said, "Has Lao Ning pockmarks?" How we all laughed.

The mistress was also a woman of uprightness and breeding. Her father had been a Tao T'ai, an Intendant of Circuit. She was a good mistress. When she saw that the meat provided for us by the cook was not sufficient she would slip a few extra cash to me and say, "Here, go and buy yourself something to eat." Or she would take a preserved egg from the table and say, "Here, cook this and eat it."

My mistress told me that there were three things that I must not do.

"You must not act as a matchmaker for a girl to be a concubine. You must not act as matchmaker for a woman to marry a second husband. You must not become a Christian.

"A hall is not a room. A concubine is not a person. You must not sin in so destroying a life. To be a concubine is also to suffer too much. She is at the mercy of the first wife.

"A good horse does not carry two saddles. A good woman does not marry two husbands. To marry a second time, for a woman, is to mix the stream of life, and so it is a sin.

"The Christians teach loyalty to Heaven but they also teach people to dishonor the graves of their ancestors. And that for us is a great sin. For us, our highest loyalty is to our ancestors."

And truly my mistress was right, at least in the matter of concubines. I have never seen it work unless the first wife was dead.

There was a girl in P'englai, a daughter of one of the city elders, who was married to one of the officials as his concubine. He married her with a red chair and all the ritual of a proper wedding. On the third day when he sent her home to visit her family he sent with her the official umbrella and the baton of office and retainers carrying spears as he would have done for his wife. Everyone thought she was a very fortunate young woman and some envied her.

Then he was sent to another post. He went to his home in the south, taking her with him. Some time later her brother went south to see her and to acknowledge kinship with the family. When he got to the house the gate people asked his name and the nature of the business he had with them. Then they came out, saying that the old mistress said, "We have no relatives by that name." But as he had sat in the gatehouse waiting he had seen his sister kneeling in the court, and the rain was falling. But since she was a concubine he could do nothing.

In the family of the Inspector of Customs where I worked for a few months the master and the mistress combined against the concubine. I do not know why they hated her so. She had to wait on the mistress, take her tea and food and comb her hair and even wash her feet.

Sometimes people ask why a man does not defend the woman he has brought into the house. He is ashamed to do so. In such matters a man must listen to his wife. It is a question of face, and his face is with his wife. The rightness of things is with the wife. It has been placed with her.

Sometimes the concubines seem to have things their way but it does not work for long. There was a family that married a wife to their son. She turned out to be very ill favored, and stupid also. They could teach her nothing. At last the old people said, "She is impossible. Come, let us starve her to death." They put her in a side room and locked the door and did not give her food. But the young man was sorry for her, so each day as he ate he smuggled a couple of pieces of bread up his sleeve. We wore long wide sleeves in those days. And as he passed her window he slipped the bread in between the bars of the lattice.

When the parents went to see her and found her fat and placid they marveled. And when, watching, they found that their son was feeding her they said, "Come, if he does not find her impossible why should we despise her?" And so they let her out.

The young man was studying for the provincial examinations. One night he dreamed that a tiger walking by struck him on the chest. And he awoke very happy, feeling it to be of good omen that the king of the beasts had touched him. When fully awake he saw that his wife's hand was on his chest. He threw it off angrily and announced to the family that he was not going to take the examinations. His older brother demanded to know why. The younger brother then told the story of the dream and ended up by saying, "And when I awoke I found that it was that thing's hand upon my chest."

"Oh, but brother," said the elder, "you most assuredly must go. Your destiny is good. You would be throwing fate aside not to go. She may be ill favored but it seems that she is blessed by fortune." So the young man went and passed high in the examinations and was given an official post almost immediately. And his rise was fast and to lucrative positions.

When he became important and wealthy he took to himself two concubines at one time. As the first wife was stupid and did not know how to control them or even to protect herself, they treated her very badly and starved her. She became thinner and thinner. And he in his official life and with the two new wives did not notice.

Then one day she was invited to dinner with the wives of the other officials and they asked her why she was so thin. She told them her troubles and her inability to cope with them.

"We'll tell you what to do," said the other wives. "Next time your husband is out, you put on the official hat, take the official seal, and sit at the judgment table." The wife thanked them, saying that she could not have thought of the plan herself.

The next time her husband was out she put on the official hat and took the official seal and sat at the judgment table. And the yamen underlings said to her, "What would you that we do?"

And she said, "Fetch them."

When the concubines were brought she said, "Beat them." And they beat them with many boards.

The husband came in while the beating was being done, and with bent head he sat by the side door, for the seal was in action and he was but a man before it as any other. He then knelt to his wife who was wearing the official hat, and asked her what was the matter, and she told him of her troubles.

Arrangements were made, and that set of quarrels settled. But to avoid further trouble her husband suggested that she return to their old home and live quietly with his father and mother. So she went back, and in three months he lost his post and had to retire to his home. She was ill favored but destiny had decreed that she had fortune with her.

In such matters a man must listen to his wife.

In an argument over concubines a man cannot overcome his wife with principles because the principles are with her.

While I was in the K'ang Shih yamen my mistress invited the wives of all the officials to dinner one day. The garrison commander had left his wife at home and had married a concubine in the city. She was the daughter of a maker of bean curds. My mistress thought that as the wife was at the old home she could ask the concubine. When the wife of the assistant district magistrate saw the concubine of the garrison commander coming, she ordered her chair and left. You can imagine how badly my mistress felt.

My master and mistress were very indulgent to their daughters who always wished to have some amusement going on. Every day there had to be storytellers or blind musicians, and if nothing better offered, the peddler women's tales of their families in the city. Any excuse was good enough for an entertainment to be held. On their birthdays there had to be entertainments by trained bears and monkeys, or acrobats and jugglers. But the best liked of all entertainments was the drama. They would build a low platform at the south end of the court and then the officials and the wealthy of the city with their wives and families would come and watch. There was a porch around the court. There would be tables spread with food and drink, tables for the women on the two sides and for the men on the north veranda opposite the stage or in the guest hall. They would sit in their gay clothes and drink tea and eat savory dishes and listen to the plays. And we would serve them and listen also.

The house in which my master lived was in the north of the city near the North Gate. On that street there lived a poor scholar who had passed his first examination but had no money to study further. If the examinations had been held in any other city he could not have got his degree. He had not the money for even a short journey. He made a kind of living by writing letters for people and by teaching them when he could find one to engage him. He ate at the house of a cousin whom he called "Elder Sister," for his parents were dead.

At that time all actors were men. Women actors were beginning to be seen in the great cities but had never been seen in so provincial and conservative a place as P'englai. The prefect, who was from the capital and very fond of the theater, had asked a troop of women players to come to the city. He invited all the officials and gentry of the city and members of the families of absent officials. The students and younger licentiates heard of it and they were very indignant. They wanted to come too and did not see why they were not allowed in. So they said that it was immoral to have women actors. The actresses sang and also sat with the men at table or served them while eating and amused them. The prefect was afraid to have the performance in his own house, but my master, having no official post and no seal to guard, offered to have it in his.

On the day of the performance when all the players and guests were in the compound the gates were locked and guards posted to keep the mob outside. And the mob gathered was not small; yelling and shouting and pounding on the gate, they gathered. I was on a bench near the wall. As we sat there listening to the play, suddenly something plumped on my chest and rolled into my lap. It was a big stone. More stones fell into the court. The soldiers were ordered to disperse the mob. They rushed out. The people fled, and the soldiers caught only one person and tied him to the pillar of a temple across the street for a day and a night while the people passed by and jeered. It was the young scholar, Wu P'ei-fu. He was so humiliated by this that he left the city and joined the army. That was how the great general and warlord Wu P'ei-fu got his start in life, by being driven from home.

When he was married, years afterward—he had by then got himself a post somewhere—he married a girl from one of the villages near P'englai. I saw her. She was good enough to look upon in the face, but her shoulders were too square for real beauty.

When he was married he rode in the special chair in which the Ch'eng Huang Lao-yeh, the God of the City, was carried out three times a year in procession. It was a chair open on all four sides that all might see him. It is no light thing to ride in the god's chair. It announced that he was now a prince, for the God of P'englai City had the rank of a prince. This could be seen from the princely hat he wore and from the color of his robe which was red or yellow. It is not easy to get the chair of the god to ride in. Only one with great audacity and belief in himself would dare to ask for it from the elders of the city. And he must also have spent much money.

The stories told by the women peddlers were many. The prefect, the highest civil official, was a Manchu named T'an. He had four wives and his mother living with him. His first wife took precedence over his mother because the mother had been only a concubine. When they went out in chairs the wife's chair went first and then came the mother's. The wife's chair ranked four petty officers to steady the poles when she got in and out, but the mother's ranked only four slave girls. And when they went out to formal dinners the wife sat in a higher seat than the mother.

The prefect had a friend living with him whom we called Ch'en the Rabbit Master. He had been an actor and had been the pleasure of the prefect and had then lent him money to buy his prefecture. He lived in the house as an honored guest until he was caught by the prefect in the Second Mistress' room. He ran away without his clothes, or so the story goes. The prefect sent him some clothes and he went back to Peking.

The Second Mistress had borne him two sons, but the prefect said that he could not bear to see her again and she was sent away. The sons, of course, belonged to the First Mistress.

The prefect said, "I cannot lift my head. My hat is too heavy."

One day my mistress lost her little dog. It was a Pekinese and she was very fond of it. So she sent me to the fortune-teller to find out where it was.

The yamen where my master lived was near the North

Gate of the city. Just inside the North Gate on the main street there was a small temple in which lived a Taoist priest. He had a hunchbacked wife and several children. And although he burned incense whenever the God of the City was carried by and prostrated himself to the ground, he was not a good man. There was a little girl who used to buy sweets from his stand and so got friendly with him. He took advantage of her one day when his wife was not at home. I saw the child afterward in her own home. It was a very wicked thing that he had done to her. But the family was poor so there was no one to tell the magistrates.

As well as burning incense and selling fruit and sweets in front of his temple door, under the big tree, he also had a fortunetelling table. When the little dog was lost my mistress sent me to this priest to find out where it was. He consulted his books and his diagrams and told me that it would be home the next day. And the next day he brought it back himself and got the reward. He had seen the little dog and knew where it was.

No fortuneteller has ever told me what was going to happen. One told me that I was to die the next year. That was many years ago. Another told me that I would marry man after man and that with each I would have worse luck than even with my old opium sot.

Not all fortunetellers have the real power, but some have. An old woman dreamed a dream. She dreamed that she took a pear, cut it in half, and she and her husband ate it. The next day she went to the soothsayer and asked him for the meaning of the dream. The soothsayer was Chou Kung. He told her that her son would surely die. The old woman wept, and weeping started for home. She wept so loudly that the Holy Maiden, T'ung Hsien Nu, who walks with the Immortals, heard her and sent a slave girl to ask what was the matter. On hearing the old woman's tale she said, "He can foretell the future but I can untie the future. Your son will not die. Go home, get a cock, take him in your arms, and patting him call your son by name."

The old woman did as she was told, took the cock in her arms, and walking around the court and in the rooms, called, "My son, O my son, come to me, my son."

The son had been on his way home when overtaken by a rainstorm. He saw an old brick kiln and went in for shelter. While there he heard his mother calling him and went out into the rain to see her, and as he left the kiln it fell in. If he had been there he would have been buried and killed.

When he got home and his mother heard the tale she went to Chou Kung and said to him, "You did not tell the truth. My son came home alive."

"That cannot be," said Chou Kung. "He must surely have died. It is written clearly in the ideographs of his life. It is his fate."

But when the mother had told him all, he said, "It is that maiden again, and she has spoiled my readings of destiny."

There are many stories of the deeds of these two and of their ability to foretell the future and of her ability to influence it. So he sent messengers to ask her in marriage that he might by taking her virginity destroy her power and bring it under control of his. And the way to do this was to get her *sha*, which is part of the power of her spirit.

The sha is a very strong spirit. There was a family who had decided on the day for the marriage of the son. When the day came he was very ill, but in spite of this the mother said that they would bring home the bride. The mother was not a woman with a good heart. As the wedding chairs were ready to start for the bride the boy breathed his last. They covered him with a quilt and the mother herself went to fetch the bride home. When the bride came to the house they led her into the bridal chamber and told her that her husband was ill and that he had just taken medicine to make him sweat, so that she must not disturb him or un-cover him. Then they shut the door and left them there. Like a dutiful wife she said, "Don't disturb yourself. Lie still and sweat."

In the night the sha came. It always returns after death. The geomancers can tell when it will return and the family leave the house and avoid it. The sha came. The young wife suddenly saw two roosters, a white one and a red one, fight-ing on the floor by the k'ang. And she thought, "Where did these creatures come from with the door shut?" She watched them fighting on the floor until she was fright-ened. So she shook her husband and called on him to awake and see what was the meaning of the strange sight. And as she shook him he drew a long, gasping breath. The white rooster entered his body and he sat up alive. She rushed to the door to call her mother-in-law, and as the doors were opened the red rooster ran out and escaped. The mother-in-law died.

Two women were living together, a mother-in-law and a daughter-in-law. The son had been gone for ten years. They had a very hard time to get enough on which to live. The neighbors suggested many times that the young woman should marry again. They said, "You will then have enough to eat and your old mother can live for a long time on the marriage money."

But the young woman always said, "I cannot leave my mother-in-law."

So they began to talk to the old woman and she talked to the young one, and the young one wept and said that she would not go. But the old one was insistent.

"Why should we two starve here together?"

At last the young woman said, "If we are sure he is dead I will go forward."

So they went to a fortuneteller and asked if the man was alive. They gave the fortuneteller his eight ideographs, the ones controlling his destiny, the ideographs of the hour, the day, the month, and the year of his birth. The fortuneteller made his calculations and he said, "His fate is the earth fate for this year and time. The earth element covers him. He is surely dead."

Then they lifted their voices and wept and begged him to reckon the books again and see if there was no other interpretation.

So again he searched his books and again he said, "He is dead." And the women wept.

"If it is not true you may come and overturn my table and destroy my books and my table of divination."

Across the street under the temple wall there was another fortuneteller. Seeing and hearing their grief he said, to comfort them, "There may be another interpretation. Perhaps he is journeying toward you and that is why he is covered with dust, the dust of travel."

With renewed hope the women started home. When nearing their house the neighbors came out to see them and said, "Do you know that such and such a one has come?"

The two women turned around immediately, and before going home to see their son and husband they went to the fortuneteller and overturned his table and destroyed his books.

I saw many interesting things when I lived in the families of the civil officials. There were many festivals and holidays and we enjoyed them.

The New Year began when the farmer had finished his work and was ready to start on his new cycle of labors, and the New Year holidays were his breathing space between. Sometimes the first day of spring was the first day of the year. It must have been meant by the old people to be so always. While the months follow the moon and New Year's day depends on its waxing and waning, planting and harvest time depend on the warmth of summer and the cold of winter, on the length of the shadow cast when the sun shines, and on the part of the sky the sun crosses.

The imperial astronomers work all the year with their calculations to keep the two systems of festivals, those governed by the moon and those governed by the sun, as clear in their relationships as they can. For besides the first day of spring there is also the winter solstice and the summer solstice with which it must be kept in harmony. When they have finished their calculations for the year, the results are printed in the imperial almanac which is sold in every bookshop and hawked in every street of every city.

But whether spring started a few days before or a few days after the day on which the New Year began, it was one of the gayest of all the gay days of the holidays, for it was the day on which the Spring Bull was met.

He is met by the whole city. The people flock out of the East Gate of the city to the outskirts of the east suburb. They are dressed in their New Year clothes, their newest and their gayest clothes. They flock out to see each other, to see the crowds. And they flock out to see the officials of the town. For all the officials must go to meet the bull and escort him back to the city. They are dressed each in the official robes of his rank, embroidered coats or armor mounted on gay-colored cloth. They wear their official hats with the red tassels and the peacock feathers or the high-winged helmets. They go on horseback or in chairs, preceded by horsemen and gongs and umbrellas and followed by horsemen. Each official moves in a gay and noisy cavalcade.

But above all the people go out to see the Spring Bull, to meet him, and to bring him home. They do not know where he comes from. It is enough that he comes from the east and they meet him and bring him home. Crowding around the bull's escort and those of the officials, they bring him home on a river of people. The great bull is carried high on a sedan-chair platform. In P'englai he is carried by sixteen men, for he is royal, he is imperial, he is Sui Yang Ti, the ancient emperor himself. Beside him is carried his nephew Yang Mang who the people say lost the empire for his family by his perverse disposition. When his father told him to go east he went west. When his father told him to go west he went east. His father wanted to be buried in the valley so he told Yang Mang to bury him on the mountain top. Yang Mang said, "This once will I obey my father; never have I done so before." And thus was all the fortune of the family blown away.

The procession passes through the main streets whose shops are boarded up for the holidays. The people crowd close. Each man wants to see for himself what color the bull is this year, for by the color they know what to expect of the year. If he is white it will be a year of mourning. If he is black it will be a year of plague and sickness. If he is red there will be disaster by fire. If he is yellow the people rejoice, for the year will be one of plenty and prosperity for all. But seldom is he of one color. His head may be black and his horns white. He may have a yellow back with a great red patch on it. His color is determined by the board of rites in the capital, by the imperial geomancers.

They bring him to the yamen of the prefect. They take him into the great court. The cannon are fired and a string of firecrackers set off. Yang Mang lifts his paper arm and strikes his uncle, the paper bull, the emperor Sui Yang Ti, with his whip. It is a signal. The people rush upon the bull. They beat him to pieces. They tear him to tiny bits. Whoever gets a piece of the bull is a lucky man. It is most lucky to get the head. He who gets the head takes it to the nearest pawnshop and is given five hundred cash.

There came to me one day when I was working for the Ch'ien family a matron of my husband's village. Her husband was a scholar. and a doctor and a man of note and

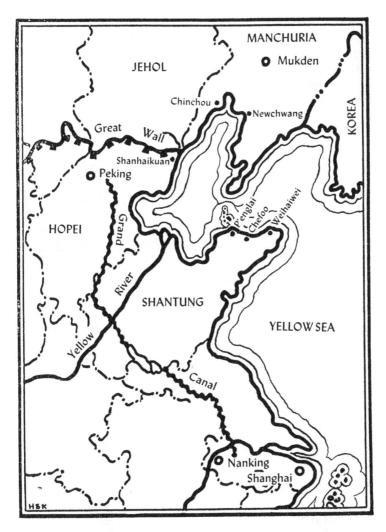

WHERE LAO T'AI-T'AI LIVED AND TRAVELED

he had a son who was also a scholar and a doctor but he was of a generation lower than my husband so he called my husband uncle. The daughter of the family was to be married to a young man who was an officer in the camp with General Sung Ch'ing in Manchuria. He could not come home for his bride and wanted her sent to him. The bride's mother could not go. There were serving maids and there were slave girls to go with the bride, for they were wealthy, but someone there must be to take charge of them and also there must be someone to represent the women of the family. The bride was six years younger than I and she called me grandmother because my husband was of her grandfather's generation. So they asked me to go.

My mistress said that I could go and that she would take care of Mantze for me while I was away. She gave orders to the servants that they were not to beat Mantze or in any way mistreat her—that she was to be as the daughter of my mistress. Always I was one that liked to see new places and to see new people. So we started.

We went by mule litter to Chefoo and it took two days across the hills and along the banks of the sandy rivers. This was my first trip to Chefoo. There I rode in rickshas pulled by men for the first time in my life. We boarded a steamer. We had a stateroom. We were all very sick, the bride and the maids and the slave girls and I. Each that was better for a time waited on the others. Mostly it was I who waited on them, for the Heavenly Grandfather has given me a strong body. We were in the steamer for seven days, for there was a great storm. When we landed at Newchwang in Manchuria we climbed down the side of the boat with chains around our waists. And always as we traveled I was thinking of my daughter.

General Sung and his army were at Chinchou, so we got off the boat at Shanhaikuan. Then for five days we traveled in freight carts, going north and east. The roads were very rough indeed. They were so rough that at times we had to cling to the bamboo framework on which the mat covering of the cart was stretched to keep from falling out. We tied towels to the top of the frame and swung from them to ease the bumping.

There was a great wedding and great sights to be seen. For a month we rode around on horseback to see the relatives. But after the wedding I wished to go home. They begged me to stay and live with them. I said that I could not, that my child was at home, that I was homesick for her, and that I must go to her. They said that they would send for her and bring her to me. But I thought of all the misery of seasickness that I had endured and of the labors of the journey, and that it was all more than her young body would be able to stand. And besides I was homesick for the land to which I was accustomed. The people in Manchuria did not talk as our people talked, nor did they eat the same food. I said that I would go.

The wife of one of the officers was going back, and I arranged to go with her. We took passage on a junk. There was one small cabin only, with a mat dividing it in two, and we had one of the halves. For nine days we lay and suffered in that hole. There was room only for the two of us to lie side by side, and always we were sick.

On the fifth day we got to Newchwang and the harbor was full of floating corpses. Our boat passed through a sea of corpses as thick as goldfish in a pond where a piece of bread has been thrown. We pushed our way through the corpses, and the dead bodies floated against the sides of our boat. They were swollen, and the trousers had washed off. Their buttocks pushed out of the water and their queues had become unbraided and their hair was washing around their heads. The ankle straps of their trousers had not come undone, but the accident had come at night while they were sleeping, so their belts had not been fas-

tened. Their black trousers had washed out from their
ankles. They were black, swollen bodies like dressed pigs,
with black streamers floating from each end. They were
not good to look upon.

I decided in my heart that I would never sleep on a boat
without first tying the sash of my trousers firmly and binding my hair. I would not be such a corpse.

They told us that a gunboat had been starting out to
subdue a Mohammedan rebellion and that the boiler had
burst. The bodies were those of soldiers.

The rebellion had come about in this wise. The Japanese
and the English and the Russians were all mixed up in it
in some way that I could not understand. There was fighting. It was at the same time that the Japanese had dropped
shells over P'englai. When the fighting was all over the
Japanese got Formosa and the Russians got Port Arthur
and the English got Weihaiwei which the Japanese had
taken from us the winter they had shelled P'englai.

During this war a relative of my master Li the Nieh
T'ai had been killed. He was a man named Tso, and was
called Chu-k'uei. He was the official in charge of the imperial tombs in Mukden—no small post. In the fighting
he was blown away. They never found anything of him.
There was talk of a leg which someone said was his, but they
never could be sure. Whether it was the English or the
Russians or the Japanese who did it I do not know, but his
wife was very angry about it, and she was a woman of ability. She went to the Empress Dowager and demanded
soldiers to lead against the foreigners. The Empress
Dowager would not grant her request.

The Li family and the Tso family were Mohammedans,
and the Mohammedans are all very fierce and revengeful.
Madam Tso went to the place where the Mohammedans
lived and raised a rebellion among them. The Chinese
gathered troops to put down the rebellion. They put the

troops on a boat to send them to the place of the rebellion.
Before the boat even left the harbor the boilers burst and
there was never talk of another expedition.

It was on this journey that I learned to smoke. I was
homesick and lonely for my child, and so I learned to smoke.
The young mistress had a water pipe and she would let me
smoke it when I pleased. When I left she gave the pipe to
me.

It took us four days to get from Newchwang to Chefoo.
When we got to Chefoo I felt that I was home again, and
when we came in sight of the hills of P'englai the gates of
my heart opened.

It was soon after my return from Manchuria that my
master fell ill. There were other causes for his illness and
for his death, but it was the shame of his daughter that did
most toward killing him.

He was sent by the prefect to Lai Yang district to look
into a matter of gambling, to catch and punish the gam-
blers. They were gambling in the district yamen itself, it
was reported.

The prefect wished to look over the district accounts and
to talk them over with the district magistrate. But the
magistrate would not come. The books had been hidden by
the city elders. And so a lawsuit started. Ch'ien Lao-yeh
was sent to sit in judgment. The Lai Yang district magistrate became very angry indeed and he made a straw man
and two servants of straw. On each one he put a name. He
beat the straw men with sticks and then he burned them.
Ch'ien Lao-yeh was ill for many days.

The feud between the Lai Yang district magistrate and
the city elders was so great that they fought it even to the
capital, and all were in prison many years because of it.

The old master and the mistress were people of uprightness and of breeding. But truly the two Ch'ien girls were
not good. The elder one was better than her sister. A

mother-in-law had been arranged for her, so she did not do what she should not do. But the younger did what was wrong. Whenever we came to the younger girl's room we had always to cough or to make some other noise to warn him who was there. He was the young boy who managed the house for them, and had been brought up in the family. Everyone knew about this except the old master and the old mistress. Many had lost their jobs trying to warn them. The master and the mistress could both read, so someone would write words on pieces of paper and leave them to be found under the tea cups. But always someone lost a job whenever this happened.

One day a servant came in asking the mistress if she wanted any "stinking eggs." This was the name given in the western part of the province to preserved eggs. In our part of the province they were called "transformed" eggs. One of the daughters became very angry.

"Mother," she said, "do you not see that the servant is reviling us?" A woman of no virtue is often called a rotten egg. So we gave up trying to warn the master and the mistress.

They had doctors come to see the girl. The servants all knew about it, even to the gatehouse and beyond. Those on the street knew about it, but the old master and the mistress did not know what was the matter. They even asked the foreign doctor to come, and so the foreigners knew about it. When he came we asked him not to give her too strong a medicine, for we did not wish her to suffer. And so he gave her a little something that did not matter.

She became very ill and the whole family gathered around her. I held her in my arms. Her father and her mother, her sister and her cousin, the son of her father's brother, were there. They thought she was dying.

Then the baby was born into her clothes and when they heard it cry, then only did they know what had ailed her.

The old mistress said to me, "Take it away." And just as it was in her clothes I took it, wrapped in the clothes into which it had been born, and took it to the house of my sworn mother.

When I returned the gateman wanted to know how much they had given me to take it away. He said, "How much did they give you to carry it away?"

And I said "Nothing."

"Nothing?" he said. "I thought that at least they had weighted the bundle with a few taels of silver or I should have challenged you as you went out and demanded to see what you were stealing from our master. Then there would have been a scandal of large proportions." But he was my friend and so nothing came of it.

They sent the boy away, but after he left the second daughter began to see too much of her cousin.

The younger daughter was not the only one among the official families who did not lead a regular life. In another yamen was a girl who slept with whom she would. She slept even with the monks from the temples. In those days for a monk to enter a private house was a disgrace and against the law.

Even at funerals when the monks came to say the prayers for the dead they did not come into the family court where the coffin was placed except in the third watch of the night when all the family were shut in their own rooms. During the day they said the prayers in the reception room in the outer court beyond the second gate or in a mat shed built for them on the street between two p'ailos of poles and cloth built at either end of the street.

That girl who lay with monks had many illegitimate children. One of her affairs was the cause of a scandal. It was with a steward in the house, and the girl's mother found out and accused him before the district magistrate. For her face, she used other words. She said that he had stolen goods belonging to the family. The magistrate heard the case first without letting the mother into the inner court. He found out the truth, and giving the man fifty taels of silver, told him to be on his way and sent him out the side door. When he let the mother into the judgment hall she demanded the servant. The magistrate told her that he was in the lower dungeons. So she went away satisfied.

But in the Ch'ien family the father died of anger and disgrace. Nor did the girl herself have a good death. There was no son in the family, so a nephew from the south came to take charge of the funeral and wind up their affairs. He would not forgive the girl, and demanded her father's life from her. He so pushed her with his demands that she was forced to die by her own hands. But that was after they had left P'englai and returned to the family home in Hsiao Hsing.

I stayed with the Ch'ien family for three years. Mantze was twelve when I went and fifteen when I left, and they were good to me. But I could not stay, for my daughter's sake. It was not a good place for her. Mrs. Burns, the missionary's wife, had been after me for some time to go to her. So when she sent for me again I determined to go.

I said to my mistress, "My old opium sot is ill. They have sent for me."

And she said, "Is he very ill?"

And I said that he was, and that I might not be able to return for a few days. She said that would be all right, and so I went to Mrs. Burns's house.

I went to Mrs. Burns and told her that I would work for her. I worked there for two days, and when the rate was settled and the work I should do was agreed upon I went back to see my mistress and told her that I had another job. I told her that my daughter was now approaching womanhood and that she should have some training in the keeping of a home, that she should learn to sew and cook that she might go to a mother-in-law. How could she learn these things in a yamen where the food was brought, ready cooked, to her, and when she wanted anything she could take it or buy it, with no chance to cook or to sew? So my mistress let me go.

My mistress was very kind to me and did not want to see me leave. She said to me, "When the master gets a real post I will send for you and you shall come back to me." But he never got a real post. He died of anger. Fortunately there had been the great Ting family lawsuit which had brought my master about two thousand taels of silver, and that took the family back to the old home and buried him.

If my master, who was a small one among the officials of the province, got that much from the Ting lawsuit, what must the others have got? That lawsuit ruined the Ting family and they had been considered the wealthiest family in that end of the province.

The Ting family was the wealthiest family in the Huang district. They had been wealthy for over six hundred years, even before the Ch'i family in P'englai became wealthy. And the story of their wealth and the beginnings of it were often told by the old people.

A phoenix rested on a tree and the whole neighborhood came to see. And when the phoenix flew away they cut down the tree and parceled it out, branch by branch, twig by twig. They even dug out the root and took that away. But no fortune came to any.

That winter famine refugees came to the village. There were among them a sick old man and a woman, his daughter-in-law, about to have a child. So the villagers got together and built a shed over the hole made in the ground where the root of the tree was taken out and arranged the hole as a place for them to live. There the old man died and the baby boy was born.

They had no place to bury the old man, so they left him

in the hole and covered him over and then they rented a room in the village for the woman and the child. The baby grew into a great-sized man, and they called him Ting Ta Han-tze, Ting the Great Son of Han. He lived in a tumbled-down house and kept himself alive by picking up grass for the villagers to burn and by doing odd jobs and even by begging.

The richest family of the village was the family of Wang. They had a daughter of whom they were so fond that they had refused every offer of marriage made for her. This did not suit the maiden. The next New Year, when the altar was set up for worship of the ancestors, she seated herself on the altar. This was to say to her father, "You have made me an ornament in the family, an object of art to delight yourselves, a thing to be worshiped and not for use."

And when the father saw her a great wrath rose in him. "Go," he said to the servants. "Fetch a beggar here. She shall have her husband."

The servants went out. They did not dare do else. But they said to one another, "Has not Ting Ta Han-tze been a beggar?"

So they went out to find him and they met him as he was going along the road to pick up grass.

"How would you like a wife?" they said.

"What talk is that," said he, "to such as I?"

"But we are talking talk that has meaning."

"Ha!" said he. "What woman would come with me?"

"The daughter of our master."

"Now I know that you are not saying words that have meaning."

"Come," said the servants, "and drink a pot of wine with us. You will see whether we talk sense or not."

When they got back to the house the Old Master Wang asked, "Have you got the man?"

And they said, "Here he is."

They brought forward Ting Ta Han-tze. And the maiden, who had gathered together a bundle of clothes, came out and joined him and went with him to his broken house. Together they kowtowed to Heaven and Earth and lived together.

And every day he went out to gather grass and sell it, and every day they ate what he bought with the money.

At last one day she said, "Is this the only way you have to earn money? Can you not think of some other way that will bring in more money?"

"Any other way would need capital. What chance have I to gather together any capital?"

So she took from her belt two taels of silver that she had brought with her from her home and said, "Take these and start a business."

"What are those?" he said.

"Silver," said she. "Do you not know silver when you see it?"

"If that is the silver of which everyone talks I know where there is an abundance." She gave him his basket and his grass rake and told him to go quickly and get some. In the evening he came home with a basket of silver. So day by day he went back and forth to the hills until the inside room of their broken little house was full to the ceiling.

One day in the New Year holidays Old Mistress Wang said to her steward, "Even if her father is angry with her it is no reason why I should let her suffer want. Take these taels of silver to her and give her my greetings."

So the servant went, but when he offered the money to the young woman she said, "We do not need my mother's money. We have more than enough." And he being a trusted servant she took him to the room and showed him the great pile like a mountain. He was dumbfounded. And so was Old Mistress Wang, who would not believe until she had seen it with her own eyes.

And that is the beginning of the wealth of the great Ting family. It was all because the old man, the grandfather, was buried under the phoenix tree.

This was the family that had the lawsuit which gave my master money enough for his funeral and home going. The lawsuit was with the Jui family, and it happened in this wise.

The mother of Ting the Fifth was a young widow. Every day she had a blind musician come in to tell tales to amuse her, and they became very intimate, so that there was much talk, but not openly, for she was rich. When the baby was born it was carried secretly out the back gate and openly in by the front. This had all been arranged, an old woman carrying a bundle out of the back gate and another old woman begging the rich woman to have mercy on an orphan child at the front gate.

The child was brought up in name as a slave girl, but she was treated exceedingly well, and all knew who she was in reality. When she came of marriageable age a husband of good family was got for her, and the old lady managed to transfer much land and goods to the young couple, and the son could say nothing. But when the old lady died he made trouble. Before she died she had given the young couple, a draft on the Ting banks for ten thousand taels. The son claimed, when they came to cash it, that it was stolen, and took the girl and her husband to law. The accusation was "a trusted servant despoiling the master." If my master, so small an official, got several thousand taels out of it, the Ting family must have spent more on the lawsuit than the ten thousand taels in question. There were the two magistrates of the two districts and their assistants, to say nothing of the prefect and the treasurer and the judge and many others.

So the old people say that the "official has ten roads" to wealth and few others have even one. They also say:

"The gates of the yamen face south,
If you have right but no money beware of entering."

When my master fell ill of the anger caused by his daughter's actions, they sent for me to go and nurse him, but I sent word that I could not go. I was just becoming established in my new work. Then he died and they sent for me and I went. In the daytime I worked for Mrs. Burns, taking care of her baby, and at night I worked for my old mistress, helping her to prepare for the moving of the body to the South and the moving of the family. In the early morning I would return to my house and sleep a few hours.

It was then that one morning I had a great fright. I was walking home along the river bed. It was barely light enough to see. Suddenly I heard a great noise of rushing and roaring. The sensation was that of an earthquake and I saw a great mass pass over my head and land in the fields beyond. The mass was followed by a trail of smaller masses. I was frightened and cowered to the earth. Mr. Burns said it was a stone from a star, and he put a piece of it in a room which he called a museum, in the school which he ran.

When all arrangements had been completed, my mistress took the master and the two daughters and returned to their old home in Hsiao Hsing to bury him in the family graveyard and to return the daughters to the family home.

Book Three. The Family

XII

TOGETHER AGAIN

1899

MY DAUGHTER Mantze was now fifteen. It was time that she learned to cook and to sew and the ways of a small house, for she must prepare to go to her mother-in-law that she might be settled in life. Also I feared that what she saw in the household of the Ch'ien family would not teach her what was right. And my old opium sot had become more dependable in his later years. He did not now take what I had laid down for a moment and sell it before I could get back. He did not now smoke opium as a regular thing, but never till he died was he entirely free of it. He still drank it also at times. That method is less expensive. The paper in which opium is wrapped is soaked and the water drunk. That is the poor man's way. But we could live together again. When the lease of the first house I had taken when we moved to the city had run out he had lived from one opium den to another. Then, when I became angry with my mistress of the K'ang Shih yamen and lost my job I had rented a house from Mrs. Chang, and he had lived there. He sold food in front of the district magistrate's yamen. Mantze cooked it for him and he loaded his baskets and spent his days in front of the magistrate's yamen. He made enough to pay for his own food and for most of his clothes. In the winter I added a garment or two as he needed them.

With each passing year my old opium sot was more dependable than he had been, but he could not talk without reviling something. It was the fault of his mother, who had not trained him to talk properly. Every other word was a word of abuse. I would say to him, "How you do talk."

And he would say, "That's the way I talk."

One day he was gathering pine cones off the floor to build the fire for cooking. We always used pine cones for our fires. That winter we were raising small chickens. My husband could not see well. He had always been one that peered. He could not raise his eyelids. He thought the little chickens were pine cones and tried to gather them up and so got his hands into their droppings. It made him angry. He began to swear. He said, "Rape this mess of dung."

Our neighbor standing in the doorway said, "Dung is not a plaything."

I laughed and said, "There you are, the two of you, contending over who shall play with and who shall rape a piece of dung."

One day my husband and I had gone to see the lanterns at New Year's time. I saw a long thing lying on the ground. It looked like an ankle band. "It is not mine," I said to myself, and went on. My husband stooped to pick it up and it was a snake. The snake was cold and could not move. It had come into the city in a bundle of pine branches that are used for burning under the stoves.

One day while we were living in the house of Mrs. Burns's cook to watch it for him, a fortuneteller said to me, "You have no fortune. Your destiny is bad. You will marry man after man but always there is bad luck for you."

He gave me such a bad fortune and I wept so hard that I thought I would die. I said to my old opium sot, "It is no use. I will never leave you since the others are even worse than you."

It was time that I thought of my daughter's marriage.

I had long determined to get a better husband for her than my parents had got for me. I would not let a professional matchmaker find a mother-in-law for her. I talked the matter around among my friends and relatives. My sister's daughter's husband said that he knew the very man. In fact I had seen him myself. He was the son of a sworn sister of my sister and I had seen him once or twice as he came or went with his mother. There were five brothers in his family, the Li family—fine upstanding young men. The oldest was dying of tuberculosis, but the second had married, and this was the third. He was a cobbler in the camp in the Water City where my sister's son-in-law was a soldier. It was practically a match among relatives, and my heart felt at peace. My daughter was twelve when I made this match. Now she was fifteen and it was time she learned to keep a house.

And so we lived together in the house I had rented from Mrs. Chang and I worked for two years for the foreigners and my daughter kept house and my old man was better than he had been and I let him sleep on my pallet again. We had not been together all those years. But now it seemed to me that we needed children. My daughter soon would be married and go away. Water poured on the ground does not return. There was no son. What would my old man and I do when we were old? Also there was no one to carry on the life stream for us.

XIII

WITH THE MISSIONARIES

1899–1902

THERE had been foreigners living in P'englai ever since I was a child. The first time I had seen the tall man with the black beard I had thought he was a devil and had squatted in the road and hid my head in my arms. But I had gradually become used to them. The gate of our house, when my mother was alive, was only a few gates away from theirs. The room I rented from Mrs. Chang, who believed in their religion, and helped them preach it, had only a wall between my court and theirs. The foreign women had visited my mother while she was alive, and they visited the official ladies while I worked with them. Mrs. Chang had asked me to arrange the visits with my mistresses. And she had suggested me to Mrs. Burns when she wanted a new amah for her baby.

In Chinese families it is the custom for the maids to live in the house of the family they serve, and the family feeds them. In foreign families it is the custom for the maids to go home at night and to eat their own food. And even if the maid was required to live on the compound of the family for whom she worked, still she ate her own food and had a room in the back court away from the family, so that there was a semblance at least of home life. So I was glad to work for a foreign family.

But it is easier to work for a Chinese family than a foreign family. In a Chinese family, the maid brings the hot water in the morning for the mistress to wash, combs her hair for her, and brings in the meals. The rest of the day is the maid's, to do with what she likes.

After each meal the servants in a Chinese family eat what is left and also what is prepared for them. In a foreign family there is the mopping of the wooden floors. I always thought that should have been a man's work, but Mrs. Burns made me do it and she made me sweep the carpet. She had to teach me how to take the heavy side strokes of the foreign broom.

Cleaning in a Chinese home is simple—sweeping up the brick-paved floor with a light broom. And the making of beds in a foreign home is very fatiguing. It is hard to please some mistresses who are particular about the making of the beds. Making a Chinese bed is simple. The bedding is folded and laid in a pile on the low bench at the end of the k'ang.

Washing in Chinese families is much simpler too. To wash twice a month is enough for the garments which are not much soiled. We washed in the river whenever we could. Clothes washed in the river water were always whiter and pleasanter to touch than those washed at home. We did not waste soap either, as the modern young people do. One piece of soap would last us several months. The day before we washed we would take the ashes of the pine branches burnt under our kitchen boilers and seep water through them as water is seeped through grain for making wine. We would rinse the clothes in this liquid, and the next day wash them in the river. They would be pleasant to the touch. We would beat them on the rocks and spread them to dry on the banks. The men's stockings and the foot wrappings of the women we would treat with starch until they were stiff and white and beautiful.

Never had I been asked to wash unclean things until I worked for the foreigner. If a Chinese woman accidentally soils her garments she rinses them out herself before she gives them to a maid to wash. It is better to use paper that can be thrown away than to use cloth that must be washed each month. Also such things we feel are private and each woman keeps such matters to herself. But Mrs. Burns did not care what she used or whose cloth. She even used her baby's diapers. That to us Chinese was very terrible. No woman will let anyone use the diaper of her son. She is afraid that his strength will be stolen away. There are those who steal the diapers of a healthy child for disappointed mothers who have no sons. They will also steal the bowl and chopsticks out of which the child eats, in the hope of having sons of their own. In the Descendant's Nest, the hole in the floor by the bed where the afterbirth of sons is buried, they bury the stolen diaper of one family and the stolen bowl and chopsticks of another, to hold the newborn child within the house. The afterbirth of girls is buried outside the window, for girls must leave home.

To work for foreigners was more difficult than to work for Chinese officials, and paid less. The only advantage was that I could live at home. I thought that I would get more money with Mrs. Burns. But though Mrs. Burns paid me three thousand cash a month and the Chinese only one thousand, I saved money with the Chinese and lost with Mrs. Burns. With my Chinese mistress I got my room, my food and that of my child, heat and water. With my wages I bought clothes and saved the tips. I had about thirty thousand cash saved, but I used it all when I started working for Mrs. Burns. I used it for getting my home established, but I got it back working for my former mistress at night when her husband died. Working for the foreigner and living at home, I had to pay rent, pay for my own food and heat and light, as well as for my clothes.

With the foreigner there was no idle moment until I went home, and then I had my own work to do. Mrs. Burns was very exacting and not always just.

She went to Chefoo on a journey and took me along to care for the baby. After we had got started and were in the inn where we had stopped for the first meal, she said, "How are you going to eat?"

I said that I did not know, that I would listen to her words.

"But did you not bring food?" she said.

"No."

"Did you not travel with your Chinese mistress into Manchuria?"

And I answered that I had. "But what she ate I ate."

Then said Mrs. Burns, "I will lend you money to buy your food."

But she gave the boy his food and I did not think this fair. And when we got to Chefoo the eating was not convenient. The missionaries lived on the top of a hill, and the food stores were all at the bottom of the hill. I did not know which shops to go to, nor did I have time to go, I was kept so busy, and so was often hungry. The boy ate with the cook of the family they were visiting, and had an easy time. I was not happy.

One day Mrs. Burns said to me, "Why is it that you are always angry since we came to Chefoo?"

And I told her and she said that such was the custom, and from one word we went to another. It was the first time I had ever passed words with her. Truly had my old mistress said that my temper was bad, and I had tried to restrain it.

But now I was truly angry, and I said, "When we get back to P'englai you can find another woman. I shall find a Chinese position." She did not think I meant it.

In Chefoo also we had had words about my sewing on Sunday. I was standing by the washhouse door sewing on a shoe sole. The boy was inside doing some ironing. The door of the washhouse was opposite the door of the chapel, and I was watching the worshipers going in. One of the missionaries saw us and told Mrs. Burns that her people were breaking the Sabbath. Mrs. Burns came over to see us. I saw her coming and slipped the sewing up the wide sleeve of my coat. Our sleeves were very wide in those days. But the boy had his back to the door and was intent on the ironing and so she caught him.

She said, "Why do you iron on Sunday?"

"Because you demand clothes."

"But I do not want them today. You must not iron today. It is the Sabbath." And so she scolded him.

She did not scold me, for she knew I was not a believer. But she had seen the sewing before I had slipped it up my sleeve, and when we got to her room she asked me not to sew on Sundays where people could see me. And I asked her why, if their God was one that could see everywhere, it should be wrong for me to sew in one place and not in another. Were the laws that were to be kept not God's laws?

Then one Sunday when I went into her room to make the bed she was mending her son's stockings. I walked around the bed to the other side where she could see that I could see, and I smiled. And she said, "Ai, but what can I do? Half his leg was showing." But she never said anything to me again about sewing on Sundays.

At that time we had not yet quarreled. But it added to my feeling, and when we did quarrel I said that I would get a Chinese position when we returned to P'englai. Like a man hanging, killed by his own weight, I insisted on quarreling. I had used all my money, two thousand cash. I had not enough to live on. We came to bitter words.

"Never since I came to China have I hated anyone so much as you."

"Never since I went out to work have I had so bad a place."

"I wanted to make of you a very useful woman."

"It is as you say. I have always been a person of no use."

Mrs. Burns did not think I meant it, but when we got back to P'englai I went to my sworn mother and I told her my story.

"Give me a day or two," she said. And in two days she had found a very good place for me. One of the officials was leaving town and he would take me and my child, and he also had a place for my old opium sot. We would be fed and clothed and have a journey too.

I went and told Mrs. Burns, and she wept and held my arm and begged me not to go. My friends also begged me not to go so far from home. I had many debts which had to be settled and many people owed me money which I had to collect. By the time I had settled my affairs the official had gone, but I had decided to stay anyway.

I was with Mrs. Burns for about two years. While I was with Mrs. Burns we often went to see Mrs. Deemster. She it was who had visited my mother, and we all liked her. She was very sick. She had been sick for many months and could not live. Her niece who had come from America to live with her was very kind to her. She also was very fond of her.

We were all fond of the niece, the young Shao Chieh, Daughter of the House, we called her. We used to tease her and tell her that she should get married. She would giggle and scream and say, "Oh, no, I cannot get married. It would kill me. My lungs are bad."

Then we would tell her that it was all right not to be married when one is young, but when one is old it is bad not to have one's own people.

Then Mrs. Deemster died. The pain was so great that the doctor gave her too much medicine on purpose, and so she died. And the niece wept very much indeed.

The night before she was married to Mr. Wilson she

called us all up to her room and talked to us, and we teased her and said, "So you are marrying after all."

And she said, "There is no way for me but to marry." And we understood. Her aunt was dead. She had expected to live with her aunt, but now her aunt was dead.

Mrs. Wilson was always my friend. It was she who helped me when I went to Chefoo at last. She was a good woman. But I could never believe in her religion, even when she begged me to. She would make me kneel with her and pray. I could not believe her religion. But I knew she was a good woman.

When she was married she wore a white dress and he wore black. We thought that very bad. Those were mourning colors. She said that it was the custom of her country to do so. But she rode in a red chair as we did. Her husband held the poles of the chair to steady it, and gave her great honor.

The Boxer madness came to P'englai, but none were killed, nor did I see any altars. The people practiced the arts. They went through the exercises and fell in rigid spells. One would say, "I am Kuan Ping." And another, "I am Sun Ho." Another, "I am Chu Pa-chieh." It was all nonsense. I laughed at them. There were rumors of doors being marked with blood and of wells being poisoned. Rumors fell like snow in winter.

Mrs. Burns was so frightened that she ran around getting ready to leave, and fell down, hurting her knee. Dr. Deemster was worried about his fiancée. He was over sixty and had engaged himself to an old missionary in Peking over fifty. Every day he waited for the news from Peking. He said, "I don't know whether I will ever see this wife-to-be of mine or not." He did see her and married her.

In the printing house was a man named Lu. His wife had been to school and her feet were not bound. She begged me to find her a pair of old bound-footed shoes that she might wear if it came to fleeing. If any were killed it would be the women with natural feet. For a woman to have natural feet was then a sure sign of being connected with the foreigners. Old P'an, who had nursed the children of the K'ang Shih yamen, had bound feet that were very large. I borrowed an old pair of shoes from her.

Another man in the printing house started memorizing Buddhist texts so that he could quote them to the Boxers and not be known to have been with Christians. Mrs. Burns had a piece of wood that had come from the chair on which the Empress Dowager combed her hair. I do not know why but it was very precious to her. She was frightened.

I said, "There is no use to be afraid."

She said, "There is use to be afraid," and went on with her preparations.

Only the cook, Han, was not afraid. "I have never used my religion to oppress people," he said. "I have never hurt anyone through being a Christian." He went about his business unafraid. He was the only one that was not afraid.

I stayed with Mrs. Burns until the cook and I quarreled. We had been good friends at one time. I had lived, with my family, in his house to guard it for him, and his son was he who acted as brother for Mantze when she married. We quarreled and there was no way to patch that up, so I went home and became a peddler.

XIV

MANTZE'S MARRIAGE

1901

MANTZE was seventeen, and it was while I was still working for Mrs. Burns that I thought it time she was married. Also there was life in my body, and with my new family coming it was time Mantze went to her mother-in-law. Her father said that we did not have money enough to make a wedding, but I insisted. The time had come for her to marry and start her own family.

And so Mantze blames me for all the misfortunes of her life. But a woman should marry. It is the destiny of woman and her happiness to carry on the life stream. There is no way for one to plan for the future. We must take things as they come. Those who are too careful for the future only frighten themselves. All of life is in the destiny that is bound up in the eight ideographs of the time of birth—the two that control the year of birth and the two that control the month, the two for the day and the two for the hour.

And so we made a wedding for her and my friends helped. It was on the seventh day of the third month she was married. The son of Han, Mrs. Burns's cook, who was the same age as Mantze, acted as her brother and went with her to take her to her new home. I thought I had done well for her. The young man had a good post as cobbler to the troops who were stationed in the Water City. There was work and there should be food.

Seventeen days after she was married she came back again. And during those seventeen days she ate my food. I took it over to her, a basket of food today and a bundle of bread tomorrow. It was the custom in P'englai for the family of the girl to do much of the feeding of her after marriage, and even to clothe the first children. But this was more than that. On the very day that she was married and taken over to them, his father and mother left for Manchuria. They wrapped up everything in the house except the mat on the k'ang and one quilt, and went to Manchuria.

On the seventeenth day Mantze came home and I kept her. Not a cent had he brought home all that time. He was in the camp in the Water City. He got his food and three taels of silver a month. But not even a small cash with a hole in it did he bring home. I rented the east house in the court where I was living. Rents were not high in those days. For three months they lived there and I fed them. A neighbor said, "Does not your daughter's husband bring home food?"

"No," I said. "Not a bag of flour nor a measure of meal. Not a copper coin."

"And he that gets three taels and his food!"

That night when he came home I said to him, "Has not the official pay been distributed?"

He was so angry that he went away for months and we did not see nor hear of him. I gave up the side house and took my daughter back into the room with us.

At that time there was life in my body, and in the Twelfth Moon I gave birth to another daughter. It was then that we heard from him. We had a letter saying that he was a soldier for the foreigners in Tsingtao and that he got eight taels a month. Then we thought that all would be well. He would surely send home at least two taels a month.

On the fourth day after the birth of my child I got up. I went to help Mrs. Chang. There had been a death in the family. I helped them to sew white cloth on the shoes and to make the sackcloth clothing. I did not feel well.

I had returned home and was resting on the k'ang. Childbirth had this time gone hard with me. My uncle, my mother's brother, was calling on me, and the others of the family were sitting around. We were talking. There was a knock on the door and he came in, he that had been away so long and never sent us a copper coin. In those days the men shaved half the head and left only the hair at the back of the head for a queue. His hair on the part that should have been shaved was so long that it hung around his face and down to his chin. His face was black as if he had worked in a coal mine. He had on a short wadded jacket and his thinly wadded trousers came to his knees only. He sat on the bench with his head hanging and his knees shaking with cold. None spoke to him. We were all too angry. He sat there hunched in his rags. At last he said, "Well, I'd better be going."

Then I looked at my uncle and he took pity on him and said, "So, you have come home."

"Uh huh, I have come."

"I thought you were a fine soldier and working for the foreigners and getting eight taels a month for pay."

"Somebody must have written a letter to spread false tales about me."

My uncle was so disgusted that he got up. "Well, I'll see you again," he said. And he left.

"What are you going to do now?" I said to the young man.

"Stay here," and his voice was gruff.

"How can you? What room is there on this one k'ang? Already there are my daughter, your wife, I, and the child in my arms, and their father. Where is there room for you?"

"I'll lie in the kitchen god's niche."

"Yes," said I, "and with what will you cover yourself? Can we lie here under a warm cover and you lie outside without a cover? And have we an extra one that we can give you?" Then my husband took him out and found a place for him to stay.

We had some flour in the house, given to us by Mrs. Chang to pass the New Year. I said to my husband and my daughter, "He is poor and he is hungry and it is likely that he will get no chiaotze this New Year season. Let us put some kaoliang flour with the wheat flour and ask him to eat with us on the third day after the New Year." And so we asked him and he promised.

We heard later that he had been living these months in the tower over the North Gate of the city. He had been living there with Chang Chintze and Ku Ch'ingtze, black-headed barbarians, wasters like himself. Him they called Li Yuntze. They slept in the gate tower at night and walked around the city during the day.

On the second day of the New Year there was a knock on the gate. The father of my children went to see what was wanted. Before he had time to open the gate wide that man had stuck his foot into the opening. He was a strong man, that husband of my daughter. My husband could not shut the gate and so he came in. Now it is against custom for the husband of the daughter to see his wife's mother before the third day of the New Year, and so I said to him, "Why have you come this day? Did we not ask you to come on the third day?"

"I have come for my wife," he said. "I will take her away."

"And where will you take her, you that have never given her a meal of food?"

"Is she my wife or is she not my wife?" His meaning was to take her and sell her. I became angry and I scolded him. He threw off his coat and wound his little queue around his head. He squared his elbows and would have fought me.

My daughter caught me around the waist and cried, "Mother, mother. I am with you."

And I said, "Get someone to guarantee you and I will let you have my daughter, and then only."

Then my husband came and with many words got him away. But the husband of my daughter could find no one to guarantee him.

He went to see my old uncle who lived near.

"Tell my mother-in-law I can't be good. It is best to get a new owner for the woman."

"What kind of talk is this?" said my uncle. "I can't talk this talk."

I asked my uncle what he said. "He is not a person. How could I talk to him?"

"Why did you not slap him in two?"

And my neighbors came and told me that I should watch out.

One day I wished to make some calls with a neighbor. Her daughter who was fifteen said, "If you wish to go with mother I will stay with your daughter and keep her company."

So I took the baby in my arms and started out. My last words were, "Keep the gate bolt slid in place."

While I was visiting, the neighbors came running. "He has broken in and stolen." I went home.

After I had left the house he had come and knocked at the gate, and the neighbor girl had gone to the gate and he had again forced his way in. He said to his wife, "I would smoke." So they prepared the pipe for him. The little girl waited on him. He sat there smoking my water pipe, "gurgle, gurgle."

"Where is the quilt that my mother left us?"

And my daughter answered—she had some common sense—"I have pawned it for the food which you did not give me." As a matter of fact it was not pawned but it was hidden away.

"Then," said he, "I'll take this and this." And he took the big heavy quilt that we had folded on the foot of the bed and my water pipe, the one my mistress had given me in Manchuria.

The two girls began to call, "Thieves, thieves." And the neighbors began to gather.

The fifteen-year-old girl caught him around the waist and tried to stop him. But what could a fifteen-year-old girl do with so strong a man? He got away before the neighbors could stop him.

We searched the pawnshops. At last Chang the Big Head, the son-in-law of the keeper of the opium den next door, met him coming down the steps of the pawnshop on the north main street and said to him, "What are you doing here?"

And he answered, "Pai, what is that to you? What should I not be doing here?"

When we went into the shop we found that he had sold the things outright without right of redemption, so that they were lost to me.

Because of this I was afraid to leave my daughter at home. I took her to Mrs. Chang's house for three days. Mrs. Chang had a school in her house. She said, "There are many schoolboys going in and out. This is not a suitable place for a young woman. You had better find a more suitable place."

I took her to my sworn mother and hid her there.

I had some piecework at Mrs. Chang's for a few days. I locked the door of my room and my outer gate, and I put a heavy stone against the door. I went out through my neighbors' court and left the baby with them. When Mrs. Chang was through with school I went to the neighbors' to nurse my baby. They said to me, "Your baby is hungry and you are hungry. Stay here and nurse the baby and eat a bowl of gruel before you go out."

So I nursed the baby and drank a bowl of gruel. Then I went home and saw that the stone had been rolled away and the gate left open, but the door of the house was shut. Then I said, "Why should the gate be open and the house door still locked and the stone rolled away?"

Then I saw that the window was open. He had been there. He had opened my box and taken all the clothes, my uncle's clothes that I had been keeping for him, the winter clothes I had prepared for the father of my children, the wedding clothes my daughter had worn, the quilts off our bed. Everything he had rolled up and taken away.

The neighbors all came. There came so many that the street was like an open pot boiling.

I was in great distress. In my distress I thought of the son of my old mistress of the K'ang Shih yamen. The old master and the mistress were gone, but the third son was still in P'englai. He was learning to be a civil official and he knew the officers in the camp in the Water City where my daughter's husband was enrolled as a soldier.

I went to Lao P'an, the old nurse who had cared for his younger brother and sisters and with whom I had worked. She went and told him the tale. As she talked he sent out four yamen runners to catch that thing, the husband of my daughter.

And the son of my old mistress said, "Did he not eat the grain of my father's friend, General Wang, and did he not run away last autumn with three uniforms?"

Word was sent to the general in the camp and the general sent out soldiers to find him.

My husband was better in those days. He was still selling food at the entrance to the district magistrate's yamen. One told him of the matter and he came home.

Then said Chang the Big Head to him, "Are you not going to report to the magistrate that you have lost things?"

But he replied, "Why should I? My eight characters are clean." This was because he used to steal and now did not.

I had scarcely got home from telling Lao P'an when the four yamen runners came to the house to make investigation. Chang the Big Head talked to them and the neighbors talked to them and showed them. Then a small boy who sold sweets on the street said, "I saw the thief. It was not he. It was Ku Ch'ingtze."

Ku Ch'ingtze was a well-known thief in the neighborhood whom we all knew. He was one of those that had lived in the gate tower with my son-in-law. But no one knew where he now lived.

One neighbor said, "Outside the North Gate."

But another said, "Has he not a woman in the village of Pu Chia Wa outside the South Gate of the city?"

Chang the Big Head led the yamen runners to find the thief, and many of the neighbors went also.

When they got there they found the woman washing in the stream that ran in front of the house. And the woman asked them what they wanted, and they said, "We want Ku Ch'ingtze. Where is he?"

She said that she did not know, but they forced their way into the house. Ku Ch'ingtze had been sleeping. Hearing the noise he jumped up to run but could not get over the back wall fast enough. They called to him, "Where have you put the things?"

"What things?" He ran, throwing stones at them as he ran. They threw a mallet at him and struck him and caught him.

The woman's boxes were opened and there was the bundle of my clothes.

In the same hour that the civil official caught Ku Ch'ingtze and took him to the yamen of the district magistrate, the soldiers caught the other and took him to the camp.

The neighbors said to me, "He has been caught. You are his mother-in-law. You should go to the camp. You should kowtow to the general and save him."

Why should I save him? I hated him.

He was kept in the camp overnight, and in the morning I was summoned. In the camp the two generals, General Wang and General Li, both knew me. They were all my old friends. General Wang scolded the young man and said, "Why do you make so much trouble for your mother-in-law?"

The young man had been beaten five hundred strokes. Then the head of the cobblers, a man named Wang, came forward to talk peace between the young man and the general. He got the forgiveness of the general for the three uniforms that had been stolen, and persuaded the general to take the young man back in his old position. The head cobbler, Wang, went surety for him and persuaded the general to put his name back on the list. But the general said that he must first be punished and be broken of his opium habit. They shut him up in a room near the drill ground for a month. The general also required that he should join the society of the Tsai Li, a society of those who do not smoke or drink.

When he got out of prison, the man Wang brought him to me and begged me to take him back. He said many good words to me.

"Are you not happy that he is here? The habit is broken. Let us make him into a person."

"But if he comes back and still is not the material for a householder?"

"I will make him my sworn son." And so he guaranteed

him. "Let them live together and let him start a home. If there is any trouble, find me."

The man Wang rented a room for them in the Water City and bought grain for them, and they lived together. He was good for half a month. Then he became bad again. His desire for opium was even stronger than before. He stole the neighbors' things. He sold his own grain. My daughter had nothing to eat. His sworn father Wang then arranged with the grain shop to give my daughter food on account.

After three months the sworn father Wang brought my daughter back to me.

"Take your daughter. I have no way. I cannot control him."

He had been discharged from the camp and was again running the streets. He stole from whoever was good to him. He stole three measures of grain from a shop in the north suburb. He would kowtow and tell his troubles, say that he had had nothing to eat that day. "Give me a corn pone." Seeing bread he would say, "What good bread, what good bread," and snatch it and run. He stole onions from the shop of my sworn mother. He ran the streets stealing and eating.

They had been together for three months, and my daughter had conceived.

XV

CHILDREN AND GRANDCHILDREN

1902–1910

ONE night I dreamed that it was raining and that the thunder sounded. The thunder came into the room. I told Mantze to get up and shut the door but she would not get up. The thunder had struck her and she was all in flames.

Then my daughter's daughter, Su Teh, was born. It was in the home of Mrs. Lan that she was born, and not in the home of her own people.

When Mantze was about to be brought to bed of my first granddaughter she was living at my house. According to custom a child should not be born in the house of the maternal grandmother. That is not according to the rules. Even then I paid little attention to those matters. But Mrs. Lan said, "There are some extra rooms across the court from where I live. Let your daughter come there and be delivered."

"But will the foreigners allow?" I asked.

"They will not know about it," she said. "But even if they do they will not mind." It was a good group of foreigners we had there then. So my daughter went to Mrs. Lan and the baby was born. Mrs. Lan was the midwife and she cared for my daughter. My daughter stayed there for two months.

Then people began to say that perhaps now that he was a father my son-in-law would be good. He also came himself and begged me to help him. What could I do? I took him back. Su Teh was born in the Fourth Moon.

Then in the Fifth Moon the runners from the yamen came to get him and take him. He had stolen again. So we told him that he had better go to find work elsewhere. He said that he would go to Weihaiwei and that there was a boat leaving at dawn. In the night I got up to prepare him food. I cooked eggs, I warmed some bread, and started him off.

We thought he had gone. One day one of the neighbors said to me, "Has not your son-in-law gone?"

And I said, "Yes, he has gone."

"But is that not he in the cobbler's shop on the main street?"

I went to the cobbler's shop and asked, "Is Li Ming here?" Ming was his baby name, the one used in the family. His real name was Yun.

They called to the back of the shop, "Li Ming." And he came.

I said, "Why have you not gone?" He had nothing to say.

I brought him home and we consulted. "Let us send him to his parents in Manchuria." But there was no money.

Someone found him three hundred cash. We bought a big round loaf of bread, like a small cart wheel, for him and arranged with the master of a ship to take him away. The yamen runners went on board the boat and wanted to take his bedding from him and his clothes because of the things he had stolen. But my husband begged for him and said, "We all know each other. We are all friends together. He is leaving the country. Do not let him be cold."

So his clothes were saved to him, but all he could think of was the piece of bread that he hugged to his chest like the cover of a boiler, saying, "This is all I have to eat on the journey."

We know that he got to his parents, for his mother sent my daughter three feet of red cloth and a piece of flowered cloth for the baby. That was all the family ever did for my daughter and her children.

My husband said and said many times, "You made the match. You found this son-in-law. If I had made it, it would have been all my fault."

All the neighbors were pregnant that year. There was not a house in the street that had not the fullness of life in it. Even those who had not borne before bore now.

My daughter said, "You all have joy." She felt the pulse on her finger and it was jumping like the pulse in her wrist. She knew from the sign that she had become pregnant again before the first child was two months old.

The baby was born before the New Year. It was another girl.

After this birth my daughter was very ill. Her eyes were very bright. She ate twenty eggs and ten small loaves of bread and many bowls of gruel, but knew not the feeling of fullness.

From place to place I went, selling my wares, and as I went I told my troubles. My heart was full. I saw the wife of one of the most important doctors in P'englai. I had known him when I worked among the yamen. She said, "I will ask the master to see your daughter."

But I protested. I said, "He rides in a chair. How could he come to my kennel of a house?"

He came. He rode his chair to the main street and then he walked down our narrow street. He came in a big fur coat and he had on a high fur storm collar. He gave my daughter a prescription and she felt better. He would take no money for the visit nor for the medicine which we got in the medicine shop he owned.

I was again heavy with child. Mrs. Chang said to me, "All day you carry a bundle. At night you care for your granddaughter." My little daughter had died. She had the looseness of the bowels and had died.

"Your body is heavy. What if the baby should be hurt?"

I did fall in the stream that ran through the village of Shui Ching. Fortunately I had on two pairs of wadded trousers and so was not hurt. My shoes stuck in the mud and were pulled off.

By the first month I began to be afraid to go out, but I had to go out. Five days before the baby came I still went to the north street to get grain.

The baby was born. The neighbors said to my uncle, "Happiness has come."

"What is it?"

"A son."

"Oh, we cannot be that fortunate." He was very happy and so that was what he said.

And he said, "I will name him Suochutze, Locked Fast Son. We will lock the precious child to us." And he took one thousand cash and bought eggs for me.

On the eighth day I was out selling again. The neighbors said, "You will ruin your legs and your feet." But there was no other way. I had to go.

My daughter and I arranged between us. At night and in the morning I nursed the two babies, and in the day she nursed them both.

My old man was now fifty-four and he was not strong. He became ill. For a month he was ill and then he died. In these later years he had been good. But I did not miss him when he was gone. I had my son and I was happy. My house was established.

My joy in my son was so great that I said to myself, "Now that my house is established shall not my daughter's house also be established?"

So I sent to Manchuria where my daughter's husband lived with his parents and I told him to come home. He came in the fine clothes that his parents had given him. I went at night and slept with the neighbors and gave them my room.

When my daughter's child came it was another girl.

The house where we lived was near a big truck garden. The grandchildren and my son would play in the garden even as I had played when I was a child. There was a river that ran in front of the houses in that part of the city. The children loved to play on the bed of the river and to build houses with the sand and with the small rocks. We warned them in the spring and the summer to be careful, for sometimes the rain in the hills made the river rise suddenly and people were carried away by the freshets.

One day there was a great rain. It rained all night and heavily. My neighbor from across the court called to me in the night. She asked, "Have you any water in your house?"

I said that I did not think so. I sat up and dropped my legs over the side of the bed. We did not have oil in our house in those days. I dropped my legs over the side and my feet were plunged up to my knees in water. And there was a thing floating in the water. It was long and round, and it struck my leg. I screamed that there was a snake. Then I lit a match and saw it was a piece of kindling that had floated from the stove in the corner. The river which ran near the house had overflowed and all our houses were full of water.

The eldest granddaughter and the little son went to Mrs. Chang's school. On rainy days we would tell the children not to go. My son would obey me, but Su Teh would slip away when no one was looking and go to school. Mrs. Chang would be very good to her. She would keep her to lunch with them. They ate two kinds of food in the Chang family. Mr. Chang was a pastor. He ate better food. He had white bread, and meat in his vegetables. Mrs. Chang and the girls ate corn bread and had bean curd for their nourishment. They would ask Su Teh to eat with them. And sometimes Mr. Chang would give her food from his dishes. Mr. and Mrs. Chang were very good to me and mine.

Next to our house was a dairy where the cows were kept to sell milk to the foreigners and to the rich opium smokers. Beyond the dairy was the house where Mrs. Deemster lived, and next to that was Mrs. Burns's house.

My daughter's husband lived with us, but never was he of any use to anyone.

And so the years went by, and never was he of any use to anyone. When there were three girls and Su Teh was seven he again talked of selling his wife.

"Come," he said. "This is not such bad business, having girls. Each one will sell for three hundred taels and we can live on that a long time, and then I can sell you for three hundred more if there are no more girls to sell."

Then he wanted to apprentice Su Teh as a singsong girl. He reckoned that by the age of twelve she would be able to earn many hundreds of taels and all would live in luxury, and then when she was seventeen or eighteen he would sell her to a rich man as a concubine and live the rest of his life on the proceeds.

The little girl was terrified of him. She would always come and stay with me.

"I won't live with those two," she said. She ran when she saw her father.

He was working then as a cobbler, and one day the wife of the opium shopkeeper said to him, "I have here a pair of uppers that I want to have sewed onto soles. How much will you charge for the job?"

"Why," said he, "should we talk price? Are we not friends? I will do it for you for nothing."

Then she said, "That cannot be. But if you will sew the uppers onto the soles for me you shall eat with us."

So for three days he sat and sewed the shoes and ate their food. Then he said, "Now that the shoes are done they should be stretched. I will take them and stretch them." And she let him.

When, after three days, he did not come with the shoes she went out to hunt for them. She went to the cobbler's shop and she called him out and she said, "Where are the shoes?"

And he said, "That is all right; I will go and get them for you."

And she said, "You do not go alone. I go with you." She took hold of his coat and went through the streets following him. He led her into the main streets of the city where there were many people, to shame her into letting go. But she still held to his coat and followed him. Seeing that he could not shake her off he unbuttoned his coat and slipped away. She was left with the empty coat in her hands.

Then her husband took up the search and found him and said, "You must bring me those shoes."

My daughter's husband said that he would go for them, but the man said that he would go with him. They came to the house of a friend of his and knocked on the gate.

"I will go in with you," said the husband of the woman.

"No," said he. "It is a family house. The women are not up. It would not be right for you to go in and disturb them. Watch here for me. I cannot run away if you watch the gate."

So the man sat on his haunches on a little mound to see that the worthless one did not jump over the wall. The woman's husband sat there and watched and watched, and still he did not come out, and then it was noon and still he did not come out. So the woman's husband went and knocked at the gate and the woman of the house came, and he asked, "Is Li Ming here?"

And she answered, "Li Ming? He was here but he left long ago."

"Left? But I was watching at the gate."

"He left by the back gate."

From that time we never saw him again. He went to Manchuria. Friends said that they saw him there. He was sticking morphine needles into himself and his flesh was dropping off him, rotting off.

My daughter's husband was one of five sons and not one of them was any good. The first one died of consumption. The second was a gambler. The third was the father of my grandchildren. The fourth died of consumption, and the fifth was like the third. Not one became a person. They were all wasters and of ill health. It was the fault of their mother. They ran around like wild horses.

Always when their father tried to punish them their mother took their side. If he made them go without a meal she would steal food for them, take food without their father's permission. So they grew up not to know right from wrong.

What parents do not have tender feelings for their young? The old people have handed down a proverb, "The tiger does not eat his young."

But I was not brought up in the way the mother of my daughter's husband brought up her sons, and always I stayed by the way my parents had taught me. I tried to bring up my children and grandchildren in the same way.

My father was a strict man. If he caught one of us fighting on the street we were taken home and beaten for fighting before he ever talked to us to find if we should be beaten for anything else—if the right was on our side or not.

There are few parents with principles such as he had. Parents sometimes even encourage their children in taking that which does not belong to them. They think it clever of the children. When I was a child we had a neighbor whose son went out with the other children to gather grass for burning. We each had a small grass-cutting blade. He took the one belonging to a little boy. And when the little boy came weeping aloud, begging to have it back, the mother said she knew nothing of the matter. To be sure, at that time she had not seen it. But when she turned out the basket of grass her son had gathered, there was the knife. She did not return it, nor did she punish her son. She thought it clever of him. The neighbors blamed her.

Now we had another neighbor, the wife of a military officer. His little boy took what he saw, and no one ever got their property back. The mother never scolded him. She thought him clever and called it an "ability."

Truly the women of our family had hard destinies. It was written in the books of the gods. Our destinies were decided from the time that life was in our mothers' bodies.

My aunt, my mother's sister, had a business: her family owned a silver- and goldsmith shop. They had land and money. She had three daughters. The eldest was not pretty. She had pockmarks. She married into our village. She also married a Ning, but one with land and money. Her days had not much to show that one was different from another.

But the second daughter was very beautiful. She looked like a woman in a painting. There was nothing that one could see that was wrong with her. Her hair was black and thick and fitted her head like a hood. Her skin was so thin the red showed through. Her eyebrows were like willow leaves, her lips were like cherries, her nose was straight, with the slightest curve below the eyes and around the nostrils. Her feet were very tiny and well shaped. What fortuneteller, seeing such perfect symmetry, could have promised her anything but a good destiny?

She was married into a family where the father-in-law was a scholar of the first degree. But when he became old he could teach no more. Her husband could do nothing but carry a bird in its cage out for an airing and use the two pipes. Truly has opium been the curse of the lives of the women of our family.

My aunt sent food to her daughter and kept her alive, but could not send enough to keep him in opium. My aunt had even to lend her daughter clothes to come home to visit. The husband called on my aunt one day and said that his wife wished to go home for a visit. My aunt said she would send the clothes. He said that was too much trouble—why not let him take them? So she wrapped up a parcel of her daughter-in-law's clothes, even to the silver hairpins, that her daughter might come through the streets with honor. For several days they waited, expecting her to come. At last my aunt sent someone to see if she was ill. She had heard nothing of the matter. He had pawned the things for opium. My aunt redeemed the clothes, for they belonged to her daughter-in-law and could not be lost to the family.

She had two sons, this beautiful cousin of mine. The eldest had the shaking sickness and the second died when his father died. She had nothing to live on, so she was forced to marry again.

Truly there seemed to be an evil destiny for the women of my family.

When my grandfather died my father and my uncle had divided the property. So when my father went bankrupt, my uncle still had a little property but not much. He was always good to me through my years of trouble, but he could not support me. We were on friendly terms, and he always liked, when I was at home, to come and see me. He lived quite near the house I had taken.

He had an only daughter. And when he saw how badly our marriages, that of my sister and I, and of our cousins, had turned out, he said that he would know everything about a man before he gave his daughter in marriage. So he married her to the son of a neighbor who lived across the street from them. The young man was a clerk in a dry-goods store, and was doing well.

They were married and had a small daughter. That was the year of the Japanese invasion. The young man went with his friends onto the city wall to see the boats, and fell off and broke his leg. He fell from a place no higher than a man's head from the ground, but he broke his leg. A doctor was called. The doctor looked at the leg, counted his pulse, and told him that he must abstain from the marriage bed and from certain foods.

I do not know which he did of the things he should not have done, but his leg swelled. It swelled so that the bamboo splint was wrapped in the flesh of the leg. The foreign doctor was called, and his leg had to be cut off. So that always he hopped on three legs the rest of his life. He could no more be a clerk in the store. He and his brothers opened a store of their own. But this failed. They sold what little property was left and came home with their children to live with my uncle.

He and his wife had stayed apart for many years, but at last had come together again and had two more children, daughters. It was one of these that was spoiled by the Taoist monk on the north street. They also had a son. But my uncle found it hard to support so large a family. It was a good thing for them when the eldest daughter was married into a village outside the city.

My uncle had four sons. They all had asthma and they all of them died young.

Truly it is a matter of destiny. Who could have foretold that the boy who took the part of brother for my daughter when she was married would become wealthy? Who could have foretold, while he tended cows in a short wadded coat tied with a rope around the middle, that he would build himself a great house and marry a college woman for his second wife?

His father was the cook for Mrs. Burns when I worked there. Later he left Mrs. Burns and opened a milk shop for himself. The boy kept the cows for his father and took them out each day to graze. I often asked the father why he did not let the boy go to school, "Oh, he is too stupid," the father would say.

Later they moved to Chefoo and the boy was working there in a milk business and tending cows. A foreigner—I do not know who—came along and liked him. He went with this foreigner everywhere buying cattle. He became very rich. When a beef was brought before him he would say, "That one is no good." The owner would lead the animal around, and when again he brought it up to be seen there would be a piece of silver with it and it would be passed. There was also the percentage.

He became very rich and built himself a fine house in Chefoo and when his old wife died he married a girl who had graduated from college.

Truly is one's life decided by destiny. How could we tell when he was tending cows that he was a better one to marry than a man with a trade and a job?

That I was not one of the fortunate of the world was clear. While I was working for the Li family they were given a present of a bucket of turtles. I was told to take care of them.

"I am afraid that they will bite me."

"Huh. If they bite you that will be your good fortune. They bite only the fortunate." Sure enough. I put my hands in their mouths and they would not bite me.

To see a sparrow walk is also a sign of fortune. Kuan Kung saw one walk three steps. But they always hopped for me.

XVI

NEIGHBORS

1902–1911

For many years I carried a pack on my back from village to village, from street to street. This was after Mantze was married and I had left Mrs. Burns. I sold everything a woman might want—cloth, needles, thread, powder, rouge, ribbons, and many other things. And I also executed orders for those who were placed too high to be able to go out into the streets. For six years I tramped the streets of P'englai, and the villages around, and went into the gates of the homes of people of all classes. In these days it was profitable to be a woman peddler, for only woman peddlers could get into the high-class conservative homes. So I made enough for my family. But I did not make too much.

I worked hard those years, but I was at home and I was mistress of my own time, and I had many friends, and my life was good.

Every morning I got up early to buy the things that I was to sell, and then I came home to breakfast with the children. After breakfast I went to the Water City to sell. Sometimes the children went with me. The West Gate of the Water City has no tower. It was blown up by gunpowder one afternoon. No one knew whether it was the gateman stealing powder or beggars building a fire that caused the explosion.

It is not easy for a woman to walk alone in the streets of P'englai. But now I was not as young as I once was and never have I been beautiful that men turned to look at me.

Also I carried a pack on my back. I was almost as safe as when I had been a beggar and in rags.

Only once has a man followed me on the street, and that was when I was working for Mrs. Burns. She went to tea one day with my old mistress at the K'ang Shih yamen. I went along to take care of the baby. Going, I rode in the chair and carried the baby, and Mrs. Burns walked. Coming back she rode in the chair and I walked.

I had no good clothes, so I had borrowed a coat from Mrs. Ch'i, the Bible woman. In those days it was the fashion to wear coats with a wide trimming over the shoulder and down the left side, in front. So I was better dressed than usual. Perhaps that is why he followed me.

I was walking along when I heard a man calling, "Ai, ai, elder sister, ai, ai, elder sister."

So I turned and said to him, "Do you know me?"

In the days when I was a beggar I had talked with many beggars. And I had met other people, and they spoke to me, saying that they knew my father or my brother, and I would talk to them. So I asked him if he knew me. In those days a good woman did not go out alone.

He said to me many words; the only ones I could catch were "Shui Chiao."

I thought he was asking me if I was a member of the Christian religion. So I said that I was not. Then he came closer and said the words over again, and this time I heard them all. He said, "Ken wo shui chiao," which means "Sleep with me."

I was so angry that I picked up a stone. The roads around P'englai are full of stones. I picked up a stone and threw it at him with all my strength and hit him in the middle of the thigh, and I shouted at him, "Go sleep with your mother!" This was on the road outside the North Gate of the city. I have often wondered what the people thought who saw me throwing the stone.

But it was truly dangerous for a young woman to be out alone in those days. P'englai is a very conservative place, and it is still not as easy for a woman as it is in Chefoo and in Peking. When my granddaughter was in middle school and came home one summer, she went to P'englai. She and her companions wanted to do some shopping. They wanted some shoes. Not a shoe shop would let them in. The clerks stood across the fronts of the shops and held out their arms. In each place they said, "We have no shoes here."

When I told my friend Mrs. Chang about my adventure with the man who called after me she told me that no one was safe. "Look at me," she said. "I am not beautiful or even young, and yet a man followed me from church all the way to my home. I was very much frightened."

There were no brothels in P'englai. That was one of the reasons a good woman did not dare to walk abroad alone. The people of P'englai were too stingy to pay the license fees. But the women who lived in the Tung Chuang district near the back gate, north of the city, and those who lived in the Shih Pu Yi district walked out alone.

They tell of one woman whom all called Old Yang, although she was not so very old. She walked around, carrying her cash in a handkerchief hanging from her hand. She was from Chi Hsia, and the women of Chi Hsia wore wide white cuffs tied around their ankles which came almost to their knees. She wore a coat that reached to below the edge of the cuffs, and she wore no trousers. For thirty coppers she would go in with a man. For three coppers she would go in with a man. All laughed at her. She was too stupid. One day a man promised to pay her, but instead he seized her bag of coppers and ran away. She wailed all around the town. All laughed at her.

Therefore because of all these women, if a good woman goes out she must not go in gay clothing. She must wear a black coat and a black skirt and have a small black veil across her face, and she should ride on a mule. Even so she is not always safe.

A group of merchants roaming the streets saw a woman approaching on a mule. It was, they could all see, a bride, making her after-wedding calls. In our city the bride went to her own home on the third day after marriage, and then every day after that for nine days she must spend the day with some relative, her aunts, her grandmother, her sworn mother. Under the black riding clothes they could see the red wedding clothes peeping out. Under the black cloth bound around her feet they could see that the feet were small and pointed. And she rode with grace.

"Ha," said one of the men. "Here is a likely looking piece of goods. She is young. She is pretty I am sure. See her tiny little feet. I should like to sleep with her."

"Sleep with her!" said another. "You do not even dare to touch her feet."

"I would," said a third. For he saw that it was his own bride. And some of the other men saw that it was his bride and entered into the joke.

"You would not dare."

"I would. What will you give me to touch her feet?"

"Three wine feasts to include the whole company."

"Done."

And as the woman rode by, the man who was her husband went up to the side of the mule and seized her foot and fondled it. She looked down under her veil and saw that it was her husband and passed on without a word. Not until they had eaten the three wine feasts did the men tell their host the truth.

But in spite of all the very strict rules about women staying within their own gates there was the custom of gate standing. Every afternoon in the late evening the women and girls stood in the streets outside their gates or in the wide gate entrance, and watched to see what would pass by. Back of the yamen where I had worked there lived a girl of good family but not herself of good material. She used to stand in the gate alone. One day as she was standing a man passed and looked at her boldly. She fled inside the gate and shut it, shooting the bolt loudly into place so that he could hear. As soon as he had passed by she gently slid the bolt back and looked out. He turned and came back, and again she shut the gate. This angered him. He hid behind the projecting brick siding of the gate and waited for her to come out. When she came out he seized her and bit a hole in her cheek and ran away. When the girl raised a cry he was already gone and they never found him.

The customs regarding women were very strict in P'englai, stricter than in any other place. A woman could not visit on the first or the fifteenth of any month. She could not, when visiting, lean against the frame of the door. She must not stand or sit on the doorstep or even touch it in crossing. To do any of these things might give her power over the family she was visiting and so ruin them. Women were not considered clean.

No woman would be allowed in the presence of a person suffering from smallpox, for the same reason. There was danger that she was not clean at the time or that she had been lately with her husband.

It was even worse to be a widow. A widow may not marry from a home. She must go to a temple and be met there by those taking her to her new home. In the home to which she goes there are prepared a chair, an ax, and a peck measure full of kaoliang grain in which a weight has been buried. When she enters the door the chair is shaken and the ax waved in the air. This is because the word for chair

has the same sound as the word for day, and the word for
ax is the same as fortune. The meaning is, "May fortune
come on this day."

She then carries the measure of grain in her arms and
kowtows to the ancestors of her new husband.

She goes to her room, but her husband does not sleep
with her the first night. And not until the next day does he
take her to kowtow with him to his parents. After this he
may sleep with her.

When a girl marries, the ceremony of kowtowing to the
parents is on the first day, and the husband may sleep with
her when he will. The family are afraid that a widow will
push away their luck.

There were many little cat thieves in P'englai. We had
to watch all the time. They stole from me; they stole even
from those who were worse off than I. One day a thief went
into the room of some people who had nothing, not even a
cooking pot. They had dug it out of the k'ang and sold it
for food. In the hole left by the pot the people had a broken
earthen jar in which there was perhaps half a peck of
millet. When the thief came in and removed the lid he
found no pot. He felt in the hollow and found the millet.
It is a rule among thieves that they must not leave a house
empty handed. He could not carry the millet away in the
broken jar, so he took off his little jacket, a new one, and
laying it on the floor, began to pour the millet into the
jacket. The neighbors, hearing the noise, called out, asking who was there. He was so frightened that he ran and
left everything. So when the family came home they were
richer by a new coat.

Outside of the little cat thieves there were not many people who made trouble in the city. There were of course bad
people. But most of the deeds that did not sound well
were done inside the great gates. The merchants and those
who labored for their living were, for the most part, a law-

abiding and sober group. But those in the yamen of the officials, behind the great gates and in the great compounds of the wealthy, did as they pleased.

A friend of mine from Ch'ihsia, which is a poor mountainous district, said the reason that P'englai was not as wealthy as it had been was because they had been stealing the poverty of Ch'ihsia. He said this because in all the great homes and the yamen of P'englai there were cooks and tea boys from Ch'ihsia. And the men of wealth and the officials did not know the difference between these and women. They used them as such, each man with the servants in his house.

Sometimes I was called to help at a wedding or a funeral, and in that way I added to my money.

One day they came and asked me to act as maidservant for a bride. In P'englai the weddings were often at night. I never liked being up at night. I do not care how hard I work during the day, but I want to sleep at night.

At this wedding we had got the bride onto the k'ang, when I began to feel very badly. I started to go out of the door and fell across the doorstep of the bridal room.

The bridegroom called out in a loud voice, "What kind of a servant is this that you have brought with the bride?"

This he said because he was afraid my falling across the doorstep was an ill omen, and he said it to the middleman who was responsible for the bride.

But the middleman turned it, and he said, "Have we after all chosen an inauspicious day?" The day is chosen by the groom's family.

They helped me into the court and soon I was all right. I did not die as I had at the porridge station or at the Nieh T'ai's.

There is magic in words. A certain family accidentally left a knife in the wedding bed. When the bride came she saw it, but being quick of wit she picked it up and cut back and forth through the air, saying:

"Upward I cut, and across I cut, and cut the tendons of poverty. May every year be more prosperous."

And sure enough, every year the family was more prosperous than the year before.

The neighbors, seeing this, said, "We will try this method also." They left a knife on the k'ang when their bride was brought home.

When she saw it she said, "Ha! Is someone going to be murdered?" And sure enough, within the year there was a murder.

Only fortune that comes of itself will come. There is no use to seek for it.

It is good fortune to have weasels in the house. It means that the fortunes of the family are good. There was a widow Tao in our neighborhood. She had many houses but she gradually lost them. As the family fortunes went down the weasels were seen to go out in droves.

Nor is it good to snatch at fortune. It is well to take it when it comes but not to snatch at it.

One day I was called in to show my goods to a family where the daughter was to be married. I saw her. She was not beautiful, but was well grown and pleasant to look upon. A month later I heard that she was dead. She had taken opium. Her family had sold her to a wealthy man of the town for a concubine. He was over thirty and had several wives and concubines already. I do not know why she killed herself. Some said it was because the first wife was so tyrannical. Others said it was from shame at finding that she was but a concubine. I do not know. Truly had my Mistress Ch'ien said that a hall was not a room and a concubine was not a woman. In our town it was a great shame to be a concubine. Only the families that were on the edge of starvation ever gave their daughters in that way. Her family had used over four hundred thousand cash that the man had given them as "presents" for their daughter.

That would be about four hundred silver dollars now. But in those days it bought much more. For four hundred thousand cash they destroyed their daughter. It was a queer family into which she had married. They had seventy cats. Never did they allow a cat to be killed.

One day we were all called out to the street to see the marriage of a virgin to a dead man. It was a girl of the T'ien family. They had been engaged as children and the man had died before they had taken the girl to his home. The girl said that she would go to his home as she had promised. The Emperor was informed, and he granted the family permission to build a marble arch, the p'ailo of chastity, to honor her faithfulness to her betrothed. They placed it on the main highway. We saw her being taken to the home of her betrothed. She was taken in the official chair of the prefect, and the red felt strips of the district magistrate were carried for her to walk on. All the mandarins of the city walked beside her chair to do her honor. When the chair went to her home to fetch her the spirit tablet of the bridegroom was on the seat where he would have sat had he been alive. When the chair went back to the man's home the girl sat in it and held the tablet in her arms. There was no second chair as in ordinary weddings. She was dressed in black, and had a black cloth tied around her head. She was in mourning for she was marrying a dead man.

There was one other in P'englai who had done the same thing. She was now an old woman. We often saw her p'ailo. It was sixty years from the day she went over the threshold of her husband's home to the time when she went back to the home of her girlhood for a visit. All these years she had lived in one room and had never gone out of it. Nor had any male been allowed to enter, not even a male child of three years. She got her regular pension from the emperor. She was well provided for.

There are those who are truly devoted and there are those who have no stability. There was a girl near Tsinan who wept when she heard of the death of her betrothed. She untied her hair, in mourning, and letting it fly loose said that she was going to his home to be a devoted virgin wife all her life. The Emperor was memorialized and permission granted. But before the p'ailo was half built she had run away with another man.

In the Second Month we visited the graves of our ancestors and made offerings of food and bread and vegetables and meat and put many little paper flags on the mounds. If there were no little paper flags there would be no descendants for the dead. There is a homely saying, "The front of a woman's garment must be soiled and there must be paper flags on the graves of the ancestors or there are no children in the family."

It was necessary to go to the graves of the ancestors on the second of the Second Moon. After that we could go any day we liked.

One day I was not very busy. I said that I would go and weep at my mother's grave. Her grave is on the slope of the Great North Hill, about halfway up. I knelt in front of the grave and wailed for my mother. I had wailed for a time when suddenly there was a sound as of a great wing passing over my head. I looked, but there was nothing. Quickly I gathered my things together and went away. I took it to mean that my mother did not want me to weep for her. I never went back.

It is not good for those who are living to see the dead. Only the strong can do so and live.

One day as I was going out of the city gate on my way to sell goods to my customers in the Water City I met Chang Kuan-tze coming into the city driving a little donkey. The long gate tunnel is narrow, and the paving stones uneven. The load on the donkey's back was wide.

So as he went along Chang Kuan-tze was watching the donkey's steps and calling to those who walked, "Take care, take care, take care."

And I called to him as we passed, "Take care? Aren't you the driver?"

And he turned, and seeing it was I, he laughed and said, "If I had known it was you I should not even have called out."

And the next day when I had got to the house of Sui T'ai-t'ai, on my morning rounds, I heard them talking about a strange death. As I listened they said it was Chang Kuan-tze. I said it could not be Chang Kuan-tze—that I had seen him the very day before and in good health. But they said it was Chang Kuan-tze and that he had died in the fifth watch that very morning.

The day before, he had taken home the load he was driving when I saw him, and unloaded it. Then he had decided to visit the family graves. He bought some paper to burn and took a basket of food offerings and went. The Chang family, like the Ning family, had a clan graveyard. When he drew near he saw that there were many gentlemen and ladies walking around the cemetery. Being a humble member of the clan, he did not want to show himself among these grand people, so he hid on a terrace by a sunken road. He waited a while and peeped over the edge again, but saw that they were still there. He was becoming impatient, so seeing a man passing near who came from the direction of the cemetery he hailed him and said, "Do those people show any signs of leaving?"

"What people?" said the man.

"Those people in the cemetery."

"You are crazy," said the man. "There are no people in the cemetery." And he passed on.

So Chang Kuan-tze started to go to the cemetery, but when he put his head over the edge of the road he saw that they were still there, walking around, lords and ladies. He was surprised, and told himself that he would not wait any longer for them to leave, but that he would go to the grave of his wife's mother who had died not so long ago. When he got to her grave and prepared to kowtow he saw that she was sitting on the top of her own grave mound.

"What are you doing here?" he said, and sprang forward to grasp her by the arm, but she vanished.

Chang Kuan-tze went home and went to bed. He talked all afternoon and night to those who had passed on, and died in the fifth watch.

My sworn mother had a son who was a monk in one of the temples in P'englai. She came to me one day asking for help, as I knew the foreigners and those that knew foreign medicine. Her son had relations with a widow who was living with her small son. The woman was pregnant. So the son of my sworn mother had come to her, asking for help. It was bad enough for a widow to be pregnant, but to be pregnant by a monk was unthinkable. His mother asked me to help her get an abortion for the woman. I told her that the foreign doctors would not destroy life, even unborn life, but that I knew an old woman who dealt in such matters. We went to her and she gave us a prescription. We took a pound of garlic and a pound of dried crickets and made a plaster which we stuck over the woman's abdomen, covering the navel. She was to keep it on a while and then take it off. But the widow went to sleep and when she awoke a great blister the size of the plaster had arisen. So now not only had she a child inside her but a sore spot outside. She could not wear her clothes and she was put to it to find reasons to tell her neighbors. I never knew what happened to her. It was very embarrassing for her. She was living on funds that were subscribed by the public for her as a chaste widow without means of support.

I had many neighbors. The poor have many neighbors.

The amah who took care of Mrs. Burns's daughter before I came to take care of the son was a Wei Ta-sao. She
had the illness that took her into devious ways. When she
was working she was all right, but when she went home to
her family she always quarreled with her daughter-in-law
and got ill. She lived quite near me.

She would call out and say that she was a fox official
and that they must burn incense to her, or that she was a
young girl, and she would beat her own face. When she
said she was a fox her hands would be clenched into a claw
like that of a fox. Her son would beg her to release her
fingers, but she said that she could not. She was very
strong. She would jump from the k'ang so high and with
such a shout that we were all frightened. She stuck knives
into herself. I was strong in those days. I tried to hold her,
but I could not. She leapt up and we were all frightened.
We ran, and as we ran we passed through the court where
the old hunchbacked woman was fanning a portable stove
to get a fire for the evening meal. Since she was hunch-
backed she was short, and when she leaned forward looking
at the fire as she sat on the ground by the stove, she was
shorter still. She did not see us coming. We ran and Wei
Ta-sao ran after us and knocked the old woman over. Even
as I ran I saw her lying there with her arms and legs in
the air, unable to get up. But we were frightened and
ran on.

Wei Ta-sao's husband was a stone mason. She liked him
but neither of them could tell when these spells would
come on.

For that kind of sickness we know no cure. In the country districts if a child has the sickness of the spirit or is
possessed by a fox or a weasel a shaman is called in. The
shaman sits and draws in her breath in great gulps until
she is stiff and rigid, or tumbles around like a man in a
boxing bout, or jumps high into the air. I do not believe in

shamans. They have no power. They do not know when those in the court are reviling them or saying evil things about them. They are only women who have no sense of shame.

Our neighbor across the wall was a man by the surname of Ching and called Yang-k'un. His sister-in-law died in the night. Four of the family went to announce her death at the Temple of the Earth God. There was her son as the chief mourner. There was a brother-in-law to carry the incense and paper money which should be burned, and a neighbor to carry the lantern. Ching himself carried the bowl of gruel which is poured on the earth before the temple, that the soul may have food on its journey.

As it was late in the night they did not like to wake the old Taoist monk, so the ceremony was performed at the gate of the temple.

As they were burning the paper money, the gate of the temple opened and a man came out, dressed in white in the costume of a long-passed dynasty when all wore white. He had a tall hat on his head such as is sometimes worn with theatrical costumes. He came out and swept up the money and the ashes, put them in the pouch made by his clothes above the belt, and went back into the temple.

Two of the men saw him and two did not. The two who saw him died before a hundred days had passed.

I kept a small spotted dog. He was so small that in the rutting season he went mad. He was out two nights and he came home mad because he was so short he could not mate with the big bitches. He snapped at Mantze's ankles, but I picked up a stone and drove him away. He could not mate with the bitches so he attacked a pig and tried to mate with it and he bit it. The neighbors took stones and beat him to death. There was a great discussion about the pig, whether it should also be killed or not. It was something for which money had been spent. They consulted and tried remedies. They split its ear and bled it. They gave it bean oil to drink and rubbed bean oil on its ear. It got well.

Old Kuo Ta-niang who lived in the house across the court from mine was always telling me to believe in Jesus. She was a Bible woman, going from house to house to preach. She was paid three thousand cash a month by the missionaries. She would say to me, "You should believe and be grateful. See your arms and legs, good and strong, that the Good Lord gave you. Should you not be grateful?"

And I answered, "Before believing in Jesus did you not have as good a pair of arms and legs as you now have?"

She had an only son. He was no good. He quarreled with her and took opium and did not like to work. They ate bread made from kaoliang meal, black and hard. Sitting at their table she made him bow his head with her and thank the Lord for their food. Then the two took up their bread and began to gnaw. He would begin to scold, "What has your Jesus done for us?" And she would begin to persuade.

One day there was a knocking on the door. Someone had come to get her son to grind a day at the mill for them. The old woman got down on her knees and thanked the Lord for his mercies. What could you do with such a woman? Did people not come to get help in grinding whether she believed in Jesus or not? Once when preaching she got angry with a man and said, "If you get to heaven I will come up the stairs and pull you down by the legs."

A man was asked why he wanted to join the church.

"To get a piece of corn bread to eat."

Truly can I sympathize with those who have not enough to eat. Those who have never hungered know not what it is to suffer.

There was a young man of wealth. He did not give his servants time enough to eat. Always he wanted them to be with him. When they said that they were hungry and wanted to go and eat he would say, "What matter if you are hungry? Stay with me a while longer."

At last they decided to teach him a lesson. They took him to a temple fair and took no food or money with them. They looked at the sights, and always when he said that it was time to go home they said that there was something more to be seen somewhere else. So they kept him till long past the usual eating hour, and still they showed him sights, and no one brought him food and he knew not enough to ask for food. Always it had been brought to him. At last he said, "I am sick. I am very sick. I am so sick I am going to die."

And they said, "How do you feel?"

And he said, "I am sick all over and there is an ache and a gnawing at my stomach that I have never felt before."

So they took him home and gave him food, and he sat up and was well.

"That was hunger," they told him. Ever after he was more considerate of his people.

Mrs. Sun was another Bible woman who lived near to me, and often came to see me. She lived across the wall. She got three thousand cash a month, and her husband got four thousand cash. He wrote Chinese ideographs for Mr. Burns. Now their son gets four or five hundred Chinese dollars a month. But in those days they were very poor. When Mr. Sun got home in the evenings he pulled off his long coat and hugging the mill handle, ground the grain for his own family and any other that would hire him to do so for them. She mixed cornmeal with cold water and drank the water that was boiled when the corn bread was cooked on the side of the pot. She would not make a fire long enough to heat water for the mixing. Later he became a district magistrate.

Mr. Sun was a very pleasant man. When he made the

round of calls at the New Year and at festivals, leading his son, he came also to our house, although we were poor, to give us ceremonial greetings.

One night a thief came in and bound Mr. Sun's face. The daughter and the daughter-in-law were in the back, and the thief went also to them. He got eighty pieces of silver.

The house they lived in had been a house for prostitutes. One day a man went to find a prostitute and found Mrs. Sun. He was carrying a bird and a fan. When asked what he wanted, he said, "I am visiting."

So she said, "I'll make you some tea while you are waiting." And Mrs. Sun sent one of the children for their father. When he came they shut the door and beat the man. They thought afterward that the thief must have been that man.

Another Bible woman, old Madam Chu, always said to me, "Believe and you will go to heaven. Do not believe and you will go to hell." She said that heaven is a beautiful place with streets of gold and that hell is a place of torment where there are fire and worms.

My little son said, "Is not old Madam Chu wonderful! She has been to heaven and she has been to hell." Such is the heart of a child.

And some said that in heaven each one is given a crown. For each person they convert they get a gem in the crown. With no gems there is no seat for them in the assembly of the great. Is that why each one is so anxious to convert others?

Most of the converts and missionaries talked such nonsense that I could reply to them. When my old man died Mrs. Jones, for whom I sewed occasionally by the day, begged me to believe in the Heavenly Father. "But I do believe in the Heavenly Father," I said. "I have always done so. We Chinese also believe in him and burn incense to him in the temples and in our homes. But I cannot join your church." And she pressed me for reasons.

"There are three," I said. "First I cannot keep the Sabbath. I must work each day that we may eat each day."

"How much do you earn in a day of peddling?" she asked.

Thinking that she might want to offer me the sum so that I could go to church, I said quickly, "Also in your religion one must tell the truth. I cannot tell the truth. In business we cannot tell the truth. Always I am lying. If I have bought an article for three cash I must say that I have bought it for four. I must make my profit. How could I sell anything at all if I did not tell them that I was selling at cost price to them alone?" So I was able to outtalk her.

But I could not outtalk my landlady, Mrs. Chang. She was more intelligent and had a better education than the other Bible women. She said that it was what was in one's heart and in one's life that counted. She said that one could believe and still be lost if one's heart was no good. I believed what she said but could see no reason for changing my religion and becoming baptized. I saw around me those that were baptized and those that were not. There did not seem to me to be any difference in their characters or their actions. The ones that were baptized were on the pay roll of the church and the others were not. That was all the difference I could see.

P'englai City and the county were both very conservative. There was a Christian church there but those who had a home and food to eat did not join it. The members of the church were mostly from the poorer parts of Huanghsien county and from Ch'ihsia and Chimi which were poor cities in poor hilly counties. When the crops failed and there was no food it was convenient to believe.

The doctrines of the Christian religion are good enough. But those who profess do not practice them. They say one thing and do another. And what do we know of the next world? What the Chinese religion promises is as good as what the Christian religion promises. How do we know which is right?

When Mrs. Chang and her husband and children came from the country they had nothing. She taught a little school for the missionaries and got three thousand cash a month, and he was a tutor to teach them language, and got six thousand cash a month. He had a good Chinese education, but she was a very intelligent woman. She knew how to plan and to contrive. Layer by layer she raised the level of the family, until now that she is old she lives in plenty on the rent of her land and her houses. Her daughters have married well, and her son has a high position with the railroad. Her husband was a professor in Cheloo University before he retired. It was all due to her powers of managing. And she had a good heart too and was a hard worker. When she had a few cash she bought a little land—land was cheap in those days—or she bought a broken-down house. Houses also were cheap in those days.

I rented one of her houses. In the ten years I was her tenant I saw her possessions grow. It was done copper by copper. In the first years she did not let the girls eat even dry bread. It was gruel she fed them, gruel only, three meals a day. At New Year's time each was given one piece of white bread and one piece only. Their clothes were lined with pieces of cloth put together. Never did she buy cloth for a lining. But even before I left P'englai her grain bins were piled to the ceiling. And always there was wheat bread and meat to set before guests.

Step by step she went up in the world. She was always kind and just. When I went back to P'englai after having moved to Chefoo I stayed with her a week. But she was not one that made us love her as Mrs. Lan did.

Mrs. Lan also preached and she ran a small day school

for the missionaries. Her husband had been pastor in a church in the country, but he was brought down from that high place by the complaints of his people. Mrs. Lan had too difficult a disposition. It was not a bad disposition but a difficult one. She was a good woman with a warm heart. If she liked a person there was nothing good she would not do for them. But if she became jealous of a person she would hurt them at no matter what cost to herself. So she taught a small school at three thousand cash a month and he kept the gate for the mission compound at four thousand cash a month. They were given rooms to live in near the gate, by the mission.

Mrs. Lan was the more clever of the two but she would always tear down what she had built up. She liked to wear the tall hat and have a name. Now she lives with her son who has a good place in a lace company in Chefoo, but she has no money of her own to spend as has Mrs. Chang.

The first time I saw Mr. Lan I was very frightened. I thought I was seeing a devil. He would not comb his hair carefully, and it hung black around his face. He had a very big nose and mouth like the devils on the stage. He had opened the gate for me when I went to the mission compound. He was a reasonable man and wanted to live according to reason. Mr. Lan liked my uncle and often came to the house in the evenings to talk to him, and my uncle liked to visit us. Those were pleasant evenings we spent discussing everything.

The Lans had a very hard time that first winter they were in P'englai, and sometimes they were hungry. One day I found out that they had nothing in the house to eat, so I took what money I had and bought ten little loaves of bread for them. Mrs. Lan never forgot those ten little loaves of bread.

XVII

CHEFOO

1911–1921

MY DAUGHTER was a good girl until she was twenty-eight. When she said a word it was a true word, and she did what I told her to do. I was out all day, but while her father lived she was good and safe. In his last years he was quiet and orderly. But after he died and her husband went away and never returned she learned bad ways from the neighbors in the court.

It is important for the poor to have good neighbors— they live so closely. I had to be out all day and wanted someone to be in the court with my daughter and the children. I went out in the morning to buy my wares and came home to breakfast. Then I went out to sell and did not get home until night.

My daughter had always been a good girl and listened to my words. But now she reproached me for her life. She said that I had spoiled it. The new neighbors in our court became very friendly with my daughter. The woman painted her face. She cut the hair above her temples. It hung over her face in long, parted bangs. She talked all day with my daughter about pleasure. She talked and laughed pleasantly but she was not good. The things she talked about to my daughter were not good.

One day when I came home I found that my daughter had cut her front hair in the same long uneven bangs. I was very angry. I seized the bangs and said that I would tear them out, that only lewd women wore such. Good women combed their hair straight back and sensibly. My daughter answered me back and said that she was a married woman now and that she no longer needed to obey me. It was the first time she had ever answered me.

My daughter had learned to read a little and write a little, so she kept the accounts for me. Now she would not put down all the items. She began to buy things with my money and to say that I would not let her be happy. Truly it is important to have good neighbors only.

I was so unhappy I prayed to Heaven and to Earth that my sin should be on me and not on my children.

I determined to go to Chefoo. The Third Master was there, the brother of my old Master Li the Nieh T'ai, and so was Mrs. Lan; she had gone to Chefoo the year before. Her husband had died and she had a position in Chefoo teaching in one of the mission schools. There she could teach and educate her children at the same time. And Mrs. Wilson, the niece of Mrs. Deemster, the young missionary who had married while I was working for Mrs. Burns, lived in Chefoo and she was my friend. Always she had been good to me. I would go to Chefoo to a new place. I would see what a new life would do for my daughter. I had been there twice now, and it was not entirely strange to me.

Taking my son I left her and her two daughters (the second daughter had died of dysentery) and went to Chefoo to see if there was a life there for me and mine.

It was in the Fifth Moon of the year that my daughter was twenty-eight that I went to Chefoo. I got on a boat and went. When I landed on the jetty I knew not where to go. It was night. I knew only the hill on which the missionaries lived. Mrs. Wilson was living there, so I went to her. She was very good to me. The cook for one of the missionaries had his wife living in the back court. Mrs. Wilson arranged for me to stay the night with them and to eat with them. The next day I went to the east beach and stayed with Mrs. Lan. I stayed with her for one month while we hunted work. She hunted for me, and Mrs. Wilson gave me a letter to Mrs. Milikin, an Englishwoman who had started a factory for making lace. I found work there for myself and for my daughter. I sent for my daughter and she came ten days after I had come. We both worked at Mrs. Milikin's factory and got forty cents a day apiece. After the revolution money was counted in silver dollars and cents but what I earned bought me just about the same living as when I was paid in copper cash. We rented a room in the same village where Mrs. Lan lived and started a new life.

Life is like a game of chess. The paths laid out must be followed. Destiny cannot be forced. If it is forced there is always trouble.

My daughter was good again and she was good for several years.

When I went to Chefoo with Mrs. Burns I had looked for the Third Master, the brother of Li the Nieh T'ai, but had not found his house. I did not have time to hunt. When I moved to Chefoo and had time I found him. He was living well and had a good house, but there were enough maids. Why should I take the bread from another's mouth? I did not know them well anyway. So I never worked for him.

One day when I was working for Mrs. Milikin in the lace factory she sent for me and said, "Are you not a widow?" And I said that I was.

"Have you no thought to take another person?"

"I have enough to do," I said, "to support myself. Why should I add another person?"

Then she told me that Pastor Pan's wife had died and that he had many small children and wanted to marry a capable woman who would take care of them for him. I said that I could not destroy two families, mine and my daughter's, to take care of his family. She said that he was a man who could support me well, that he had land

and houses and a good position. I said that if I had had any thought of such a thing I would not have left P'englai. Mrs. Milikin's face became red.

On the way home the more I thought of it the more I wanted to do it. To marry him meant comfort and ease for me and the end of my struggles. But I could not. I would not desert my daughter and her two little children. We did not know then whether her husband was alive or dead. And I could not desert or spoil the home for my little son. I was not a prostitute that I should think only of my own comfort and ease. I must think of the future of my children and of my children's children.

They told me that Mrs. Stubbs, who ran the Missionary House where missionaries spent their holidays to be by the sea, wanted an amah. So I went there and got the job. The amah's room was large, and Mrs. Stubbs said that she did not mind if I brought all three children with me. My daughter was by then working for Mrs. Painter who had two very small children, and as she had to be ready to care for them day and night, she lived in her mistress' home, so I had her two daughters as well as my son with me. The servants' quarters of the Missionary House were large and the court was large, and it was on a hill. I thought it would be a good place for all of us.

At New Year's time the children came down with smallpox. First the granddaughter Su Teh got it. I went to tell Mrs. Stubbs. She said that because of the guests in the house I must take the sick child away, but that she would pay my wages. I wrapped the sick child in a quilt and took her in a ricksha to my room in the village. I took the two other children also. There was nothing in the room but one quilt with which I covered the three children. To make them sweat, that the flowers might come out as they should, I built a fire in the k'ang. I held Su Teh down on the bed. I pressed her down hard on the hot bed to make the heat

LAO T'AI T'AI AND HER FAMILY

Lao T'ai T'ai on the right, her daughter beside her.
Su Teh standing behind. Lao T'ai T'ai's son sitting
at her feet and the other granddaughter beside him.

take effect. She cried, but I thought that she was crying with the misery of being ill. I had burned a great patch on her hip. She has the scar to this day.

They were all ill, but Su Teh was the sickest. I thought she would die. But Mrs. Lan came to help me. She got a rooster and slit his comb. She caught the blood in a bowl of hot wine and gave it to the children to drink. That saved their lives. She also brought a piece of red cloth to hang in the doorway to keep them from being scared. It was fortunate that none of the children had convulsions, for we were too poor to have even one small piece of gold to boil for them to drink.

It was a great thing for Mrs. Lan to come to me at that time. According to custom no outside woman may come near to those who have erupted with smallpox. It would blight the children should she be unclean at the time or have lately been with her husband. But Mrs. Lan wished to serve me and she trusted me. She knew that even if things went badly with the children I would not call her to account.

They were good children but they were sick. First this one must have a drink and then that one. Always they were asking for drinks. Then that one must have the bed pan. I was busy without rest and without sleep caring for them. And I wept for them.

"I want a drink, I want a drink." Because I did not bring it quickly enough the younger granddaughter cried.

"Don't cry," said my son. "Don't you see that our mother is busy getting you a drink and that she is crying too?" They had been brought up together, and he was so young that he did not know that I was his mother and their grandmother. But always his thoughtfulness for me has made peace in my heart.

From working at the Missionary Home, I went to work at the school where the daughters of missionaries are educated. I mended their clothes and darned their stockings for them. I could work by the day and come home to care for my children at night. My daughter was still working for Mrs. Painter, caring for her babies. Our three children were going to the day schools run by the missionaries. So part, at least, of their days were cared for. But I worried because there were several hours for them to run the streets before I could get home. I had to lock the door of my room. I could not leave it open. Nor could I leave the keys with the children. They were too young.

Then one of the missionaries saw that Su Teh was a promising child and that she was too old to run the streets, so she took her into the school to board, without cost to me. Then was one part of my worry lessened.

There had been talk of the revolution while I was still in P'englai. Soon after I got to Chefoo it broke out. The police stood on the corners of the streets and cut off the queues of the men. The order had gone out that all men were to cut their queues for the Republic. My son was so frightened he hid in the fields among the stalks of the giant kaoliang. I cut his queue myself. He was but a child. If he had been caught and taken to the police quarters it would have frightened him.

An old man who had been to a pawnshop was caught and his queue cut off. He went through the streets holding his little queue out in his hands and weeping. He wept, "They have cut off my queue. They have taken my pawn ticket. They have taken my money." He said they had taken eight dollars from him, and someone gave him eight dollars. With the little queue hanging in his hands he had earned eight dollars. I do not believe that the police took that much from him.

It used to be a very terrible thing to cut the hair. It was bad luck. It meant that one had the barren destiny of a monk or a nun.

There was a woman whose husband was condemned to

die by the headsman's sword. She rushed onto the execution ground and put her arms around him, interfering with the executioner and begging for her husband's life.

"But he has sinned a death sin. He must expiate it," they told her.

"In all my life I have had nothing but the love there was between us. Let me have at least the queue to remember him by," she said. The executioner did not see through her words, so he cut off the queue and gave it to her.

Then she wrapped her arms all the tighter around her husband and said, "You cannot kill him. You cannot kill him. His sin was one to be expiated by one beheading. You cannot behead him twice." And so she saved her husband's life. He was in prison a few years, but his life was saved.

Then Mrs. Lan found a place for me to take care of a baby for a foreigner. Mrs. Yardley wanted me to live in the house. My daughter was now spending the nights at home, so I left her and the children and went to live at Mrs. Yardley's house.

It was while I was working for Mrs. Yardley that I heard again of my daughter who had been sold. A young man came often from Weihaiwei to buy goods from the shop where a friend of my son's worked. The friend of my son said to him, "Are you not the husband of so-and-so and is not Mrs. Ning the mother of your wife's body?"

The friend came to see me and told me about it. So I went to see the young man in the shop. I was dressed in my rough clothes as I always am. He brought me baskets of fruit from Weihaiwei as presents. He was a very presentable young man and he told me about my daughter. The family who had bought her from my husband had done well by her. They had taught her to do fine embroidery. They had married her, when not too old—it must have been when she was about fifteen or sixteen—for she had a daughter about the same age as my eldest daughter's first child. She had been married into a family of merchants in the city of Yung Cheng, not far from Weihaiwei. The young man, her husband, had studied for the examinations but had not passed, so he had opened a shop in his native town and sold such things as people in a small city need. It was a family that lived well.

Her husband came to see me whenever he came to Chefoo on shopping trips. He always said that I must go to see my daughter. But I could not go so long a journey.

One summer Mrs. Yardley went to Weihaiwei for her summer vacation. She took me with her. I wrote to my daughter, telling her that I was in Weihaiwei. A letter came back saying that they were very busy. There was no word that I should go or that I should not go, but how could I go after such a letter? I was but a serving woman and I wore the clothes of a serving woman. I had no money to buy smart clothes.

The next summer my daughter got cholera and died. Her "aunt," the official's wife who had bought her, sent me a message by the young man that she too was dying. She said that my daughter had been well cared for and that I was not to mourn. The young man, my daughter's husband, has never ceased to be remorseful that he did not bring my daughter and me together. So I never saw her again.

We often went to the beach in the summer evenings to get cool and to watch the fishermen bring in the nets. If I had money I could get a fresh fish for very little. One night seven fishermen who were living in a mat shed on the beach were struck by thunder. Five of them died and two lived. To be struck by thunder is a sign of great sin. It is the worst punishment the gods can give.

Always I have been afraid of thunder, ever since I was a child of six or seven. We had a garden. My brother went into the garden to get some vegetables and told me to go with him to help. The clouds thickened and the thunder started, but he told me to wait until he had finished the digging. We were getting out turnips. We started back to house and I had the mattock with which he had been digging over my shoulders. Suddenly there was a crash of thunder and the bolt struck the ground at my feet. It rolled, a ball of fire, in front of me. I was terrified. I crouched to the ground in my terror and dared not move. Always since then I have been afraid of thunder.

After a time I began to hear tales. My friends told me that I should watch my daughter. People looked at me and from their looks I knew there was something wrong and that it probably had to do with a man. One Sunday when I went home, as I went into the room, the man got up from the k'ang. He was lying sprawled on the bed and the children were all in the room. Su Teh was home for the day from the boarding school. The other granddaughter was too young to know about such things. There was also my son.

I said, "You must not let that man sleep on my bed." I could not say more because the children were before me. But when Su Teh had returned to school and the smaller one had gone out to play I scolded my daughter. The man saw the look of wrath on my face and went. I laid my hands on her to beat her. She seized my wrists and resisted me. My anger was very great. I returned to work.

Then came my friend Mrs. Lan and begged me to cast my anger aside. She said many words. "A bucket of water thrown out on the ground, a daughter married out of the house, are both gone." She urged me to forget my daughter and to let her go her own way. I listened to her words and took my son to live with me.

I lived in the big room under the front steps in Mrs. Yardley's house, and I was glad to have my son with me. The house was on a hill and there was only one other house near by where young Mrs. Stephens and her husband lived.

The cook at Mrs. Stephens' house hanged himself. Every day as I was sitting in my room under the steps sewing I would see him go by on his way home from buying the food for the day. Then one morning he did not come. They all said that he was dead. Mr. Yardley went over to see. He came back and said that the boy had hanged himself. He was no more than a boy. He was only eighteen or nineteen. He had got mixed up with his sister-in-law. She was not a good woman. Probably his brother caught them and beat him and so he hanged himself.

We all felt that he often returned. The servants were afraid to go out at night. They said that a man in white walked. I never saw him. But one day a drunken man was stumbling along the path beneath the house and shouting. Mr. Yardley went out and asked him not to shout because he would wake the baby. The drunk said that a man in a short white coat was throwing stones at him.

It is not good to see one who has hanged himself. The spirit of such a one stays around to lure someone to die that he may be released. We were all very careful not to be caught.

One day I saw a man who had hanged himself. My son and I went into the business district of Chefoo to hire a mule litter. I wanted to go back to P'englai for a visit to see my friends. Mrs. Chang's niece was also going back with us. On the way to the city we passed the corner of the wealthy walled village, the Chi-shan Suo, which had been there before the foreigners came and trade developed. We heard the sound of gongs beating. We said, "When we come back let us go to the theater."

As we were coming back, suddenly my son said, "Mother, mother, there is a hanged-himself-ghost."

I would not believe him and said, "Where would there be such in this crowded part of the city?"

He pointed up, and there was a man on the wall of the village with a rope around his neck, tied to a thorn tree. It was a strange suicide. The man was on his knees, leaning back against the rope. There did not seem to be room to hang him, and the tree was very small. It looked more to me as though he had been killed and placed there. We never knew. But we did not try to go to the theater that day, and it turned out to be in a private home anyway.

There are several places in Chefoo that always make me afraid when I pass them. I am afraid when I walk past the Customs House on the North Hill, and I am afraid when I pass the corner of the hill by the Japanese consulate. I do not know why I am afraid but I am afraid.

In P'englai I had been afraid when I passed the marble p'ailo of the Ch'i family. But in that place there was a reason—one that I knew. Old Mistress Ch'i, the mother of the general, had been a very bad-tempered old woman and she had killed many slave girls and made life so miserable for others that they had died by their own hands. Their spirits still wail around the p'ailo and so do those of the stone carvers who had built the p'ailo. She had killed them so that they should not build another as fine.

And in Weihaiwei, the summer I was there, my room was far from the house where the family lived. It was on the edge of a gully. All night there were noises. I could not sleep. The more I rolled and tossed the more noises there were, cracklings and breakings and rollings of stones. I wore out three beds in my tossing but I never saw anything.

Once in later years I had another fright. I had lent money to the man who owned the garden by the sea. He was also from P'englai and we often talked together. He sold the garden and went to live in a village at the foot of the hills. One afternoon we went to collect my money, my son and I. I was glad he was with me. We passed a well in which they said a man had drowned himself or been thrown after being murdered. Then we passed a corner of the road where I was always afraid. It was late. The night was coming. When we got home my daughter-in-law, Mei Yun, was sitting on the K'ang and sewing. She was big with child. As she sat and sewed she slipped over on the bed in a faint. I was frightened. I said to myself, "Have I really brought home an evil spirit?" But Mei Yun always faints when she is five or six months pregnant. We have learned this and that if she lies down it will soon pass over.

The Chi-shan Suo is a very wealthy village and the people are very proud. There were two old maids living there that we often heard about. They were twin sisters and their parents loved them so much that they would never find mothers-in-law for them. "They are twins. Why should they be separated. We have enough and more to keep them. We have no sons and they shall have what we have after we are gone." So the two old women lived there together on their property.

In poor families when a girl who is not married has a baby the family do the best they can. They try to find a man for the girl and give the baby to whoever will take it. But in the Suo they hold to the old tradition that the father must kill the girl. They tell of a girl in the Suo who was pregnant. Her father took her to the hills back of Chefoo to bury her alive. He began to dig holes and he spent the whole day digging holes. It seemed that he could not dig one to suit him. He would dig a hole and fill it up. He kept hoping that someone would come by and ask him why he was digging a hole, and he could give his daughter to him and so save her life. He would have given her to anyone to save her life. At last it was evening, and he saw that no one had come. So he said, "It is evident that your destiny is not a good one. You cannot be saved." And he buried her.

That is a story that is told about the people in the Suo, and shows how conservative they are and how much they think of face. I do not know whether the story is true or not. I did not see it myself nor did I know any of the people. Never yet have I seen a father kill his daughter, and I have seen more than one unmarried girl who had a baby.

One year a snake was seen in one of the valleys near Chefoo, in the stream that ran through the valley. People said that a god was visiting the place and that the waters of the stream would heal. Many people went. The sellers of incense did good business. Their stalls stretched for half a mile down the valley. The trees beside the stream were all dressed with strips of yellow cloth, thank offerings, with "Ask and you shall receive" written on them.

My daughter went. Mrs. Yardley's cook, Nientze, took my son with him. It made a pleasant holiday. I did not go. If one believes, then it is well to go. If one does not believe it is of no use. I did not believe. All that one got was a little muddy water in a bottle.

My son was in the mission school. A new regulation came out. All had been free, but now there was to be a charge of two dollars a term for English. I debated in my heart whether or not to let him study English. I had about a hundred dollars saved, but I wished to keep that for capital in case he or I wanted to start up in business or for anything that might happen. Perhaps I should have used it for him to study. He might now be a teacher and we be living more comfortably. In the end it was all used up the year that he was idle and without work. But I was afraid. I wanted to keep it. My daughter was earning fifteen dollars a month. In those days in Chefoo it was good money. I had her children. She had no expenses. I went to her and said, "What do you think of your brother studying English?"

"Why not let him study?"

"The tuition has been raised. I am afraid that I have not enough money."

"Well, how are you going to manage?"

"That is what I have come to talk over with you."

"What is it to me?" I said that I had come to her because she was my daughter. I went away with a great anger in my heart. Because of these words we were worse friends than ever.

There was also some tuition due. The missionary in charge of the school told me that I must pay the money before the next day was past. How can poor people always have money in their hands when it is needed? I was even more angry. So when Mrs. Yardley said that there was a position open in her husband's office I let my son stop his schooling and go to work. Perhaps I was wrong and spoiled my son's best chances. It seemed right then.

I worked five years for Mrs. Yardley. She had a good disposition in a way. She got a position for my son in the Customs House where her husband worked, and for that I will always be grateful. Probably she thought that she had done enough for me to get work for my son with her husband. When she raised the wages of the other servants and did not raise mine I was not happy. While I was with her I had good wages and the work was not too hard.

But the way I came to leave her was this. One day the boy had waxed the wooden floor and laid down papers for us to walk on. Mrs. Yardley went downstairs and I went down after her with the baby in my arms, carefully stepping on the papers. Then someone came in and walked carelessly on the wood and left the marks of their feet. When Mrs. Yardley came home she was very angry. She sent for me and scolded me and told me that I was bad to step on the newly waxed floor. I told her I had not done it, that I had gone out when she had and had just come back. But she said that the marks on the floor were pointed and so they must be mine. I said that the boy wore pointed shoes also. Then she told Mrs. Reed that never had she seen an amah that talked back to her as I did. Then I quarreled with the boy and told him that he was wrong.

Another time I was out back of the house when Mrs. Yardley came rushing out and told me that I had done something wrong. I was able to tell her that I had not, but her anger was not appeased. So she went into the house and told the cook that it was time for tea and scolded him because there was no boiling water. She took the poker and began to poke the fire. He said to her, "You must not poke the fire. I am baking. The cakes are in the oven and they will fall if you poke the fire." He used the informal you.

"You must not say 'you' to me."

"What shall I say to you?"

"You must not use 'you,' you must say 'Mrs. Yardley.'"

"I am an uneducated country man. I always say 'you.'"

With that she slapped his face. He caught her wrists and held her.

I came on them so and said, "Whatever in the world are you up to? Why have you hold of the mistress?"

"If I let her go she will hit me." I pulled Mrs. Yardley, and the wash coolie pulled the cook, and we managed to pull them apart.

The cook packed his things and left. He left in the middle of preparing the meal. What else could he do? He had not planned to leave. He did not want to leave, but she had left him no other path to follow. He was a good cook. Never have I seen one so good. He was clean. His kitchen was washed and scrubbed every day. And the percentage that he took from buying was very low. He rolled up his bedding and went away.

Then came a cook who knew how to get on with Mrs.

Yardley. He smiled and said "yes" to whatever she said and went his own way.

She was a good mistress in many ways but she did not know how to talk to us. When she spoke of us she used the word for bond servants.

I would say to her, "We are not bond servants, such as used to be in China and were bought with money. We are hired people. We are free to come and go." But she always spoke of us as her bond servants.

And she was always better to the new than to the old. In the Chinese teachings we say that the longer people have to do with each other the thicker becomes that which binds them together for good or ill. In a Chinese family a servant who has been with them for years is like a member of the family and his words have weight in the family and he can at times speak for the family. It was always the new with her.

When a workman came to put up the wire screens or to repair the pipes, she would take a plate of cake to him with her own hands. In the beginning when she had tea, I must also have tea. Then when the "sew amah" came—by this time there were three children and I had not time to sew— she forgot me. It was teatime. "Amah, take the children to the beach." It was hot. We could well have waited longer. I took the children and went. The sew amah was a friend of mine. When I came back I saw that Mrs. Yardley had laid aside a piece of the cake for me, but I would not eat it.

"Why do you not eat your tea?" she said.

"I am a Chinese. I have never liked your tea but as your servant I could not say so to you. I took it. We have a saying, 'When those above give, those below cannot refuse.'" Her face became very red.

She had another person in mind as amah. That I saw afterward very well. A friend of hers in Weihaiwei had gone back to England and she wanted her amah. My faults became many.

"Amah, you must not wear dirty clothes like that when you take care of my children."

"I am poor. I have not money to buy clothes," I said. "These I have and these I wear." How, in taking care of babies, can the front of one's dress not become wet at times? All those years she had not found fault with my clothes. So I understood her meaning.

I went to her room and said, "Mrs. Yardley, have you someone else in your heart that you always find fault with me? First it is the floor, and then it is my dress. I think you had better pay me what you owe me and let me go."

She paid me what she owed me and I went away. I thought that my son would lose his job also. But Mr. Yardley did not discharge him. And if it had not been that, while Mr. Yardley was on leave in England, the Chinese head wanted the job for a cousin, my son might still be there. When Mr. Yardley returned he made no effort to get my son back. Why should he? So after all it was my fault that my son did not have a permanent position in the Customs service. I would have been better to have been more patient.

After I had left Mrs. Yardley I went home to live.

I knew nothing of what had been going on there. I thought my daughter was foolish to let any man in her room and so give people a chance to talk, but I did not know how things were. I told my daughter that she was foolish and did not use her head. Why should she listen to good words that were not matched by deeds? Of what use were good words when all the rules of what is right were on the other side? The man had great boys of fifteen and sixteen running the streets, and a wife and children at home. Even if she had not had the joy of spring in her life, why did she not use her head? She had daughters only. She could marry again. What good were his words alone to her?

When I came home to live she would not cook for me. She would not talk to me. I did not know what was the matter.

One day when I was out she moved away. When I came home she had gone and taken the younger granddaughter with her. The older granddaughter was at boarding school.

I was enraged. I went to their house. I took the bowls and the plates. I threw them on the ground and they broke. I told her that never had a woman of our family so disgraced herself. I said that I would match lives with her. "I will fight you until one of us dies."

I would have laid hands on her but the neighbors came in and separated us. They sent for my friend Mrs. Lan, who came and took me away. In my rage I rolled on the ground and cursed. I said that I would go to court and accuse my daughter. But Mrs. Lan quieted me. She told me that my daughter was a married woman and so not under the control of her mother, and that the world would not hold me responsible for what she did. That even though her husband was lost and her mother-in-law in Manchuria, and although I had brought her up and supported her and cared for her all these years, the magistrate would not listen to me. It was not my family, the family of Ning, that was injured. It was the family of Li. There were none here of that name to accuse her. So I thought no more of going to the magistrate.

When I was more quiet Mrs. Lan told me that the thing had been going on for a long time and that no one had liked to tell me about it. All thought that as long as it was quiet and she did not live with him openly it could be kept from me. They did not wish to trouble me. But now my daughter and he were living together openly as husband and wife. She had taken the second step. She had followed him as her master.

Then one day Mrs. Lan told me that the matter, as far

as he was concerned, had been settled according to the custom of taking concubines. Mrs. Lan knew because her older son-in-law was cook in the same family where the man's mother was amah. Mrs. Lan's son-in-law told her that one day the man came to see his mother. He told her that he and my daughter had arranged to be man and wife, that my daughter had said that she would follow him as wife or as concubine, which she did not care, and that she would stay with him whether he had money or none, and anyway she could always earn for herself. Also he told his mother that she was bringing two daughters, the girls I had worked so hard to bring up. He already had a wife and a family of children.

For two years I did not see my daughter.

The first summer after Mantze left me I had no work, so the American missionary asked me to board two of the students who had no homes. They were classmates of my younger granddaughter's and good friends of hers. Always they wanted to go to her home to play. They had been given me in trust by the American teacher. Could I let them go to my daughter's home and see the life she was living? I told them they could not go. They cried. They were but children, both of them, twelve and thirteen. And my daughter was a good cook, her man was making good money, and she made things for them to eat. Also she is a pleasant person when she pleases to be so. They cried to go to her house. So I took them to the teacher and said that I could not take the responsibility, and she sent them to another city, to Huanghsien, to school.

As I had left Mrs. Yardley and had no place to work, my friend Mrs. Lan began to look around for me. She was teaching Chinese to a missionary, Mrs. Reed. She spoke to Mrs. Reed about me, and Mrs. Reed asked Mrs. Yardley, who said that I was a good amah but that my temper was not good.

Always it is my temper that has lost jobs for me. It has always been because of my temper that I did not stay long in one position. Always they would say that they liked me but that my mouth was not governed. I was born when my parents were older. I was their baby and they spoiled me. It was hard for me to take anything that was said against me.

When I was in service among the officials of P'englai they knew each other, as the foreign women I worked for also knew each other. "So you have Lao Ning working for you? How is she?"

"She is a good worker but her mouth speaks too fast." Always it was that way. But they liked me. If they liked me and told me that I was a good worker and a good person I was happy. I was satisfied. I did not think of money if I and mine had enough to eat. Always I was telling my children to be patient, but I was never patient myself and I would let no one get ahead of me.

Mrs. Yardley said that I was a good amah, so Mrs. Reed recommended me to Miss Mason who was now running the Missionary Home.

Miss Mason had a peculiar disposition. When I first went to her nothing was too good for me. It was, "Oh amah, you are a good amah." She would take me by the hand and pat me. But if anything went wrong she would change very quickly.

She also spoke of us as bond servants. She would pray to her god to forgive her sins and she called herself God's bond servant. And as God forgave his bond servant, so she hoped she could forgive her bond servants.

One of my duties was to wake her from her afternoon nap and take hot water in for her to wash so that she got through in time to go down to tea. She was English, and the afternoon tea was very important to her.

I worked in the sewing room at the end of the hall. But

I had no clock. So I went into her room to see if it was time to wake her.

"Amah, amah. What are you doing waking me now? This is very bad." So the next day I did not go in and was ten minutes late.

She came into my room, very angry. "Amah, amah. Why did you not wake me? I will be late for tea, and there are guests. You are a naughty amah."

But the worst trouble I had with her was the trouble of the eyeglasses.

I asked for time off to go down town to have mine mended. She said that that was not necessary. The cook could take them to town the next time he went, and I could wear hers. She took them out of her pocket and gave them to me. They were a very fine pair of bifocals. It was a pleasure to wear them.

The next day I was not feeling well. I had a headache, and so went to a neighbor's to have my temples cupped for my headache. While there, lying on the bed, I felt the glasses in my pocket, so took them out, fearing that I would lie on them and break them. The cupping took a long time and we talked about many matters. I forgot the glasses.

After I left, the little boy of the house, a boy of about nine, saw them and said to his mother, "Mother, let me take these to auntie." The children of the family called me auntie.

As he was running along the street after me, calling me and holding the glasses up in his hand, he met a man who stopped him and said, "Let me see them. What is it?" He took them into his hands, put them into his pocket, and ran away. As he had long legs he was soon out of sight. I heard the wails of the child calling me and turned.

"He took the glasses, he took the glasses." Then I was frightened. What should I do? The man was gone. He could not be caught.

It was Sunday afternoon. I knew that Miss Mason had gone to church. I went to her house and waited at the gate for her return. When she saw me she said, "Oh, amah. It is Sunday. What are you doing here?" And she was all smiles and pleasant.

But when I told her, her face changed. "They were a very valuable pair of glasses. You are a very naughty amah. You do not need to come any more."

So I went home and was very miserable indeed. She did not believe that the glasses had been stolen. She thought that I had sold them or kept them for myself. I felt pressed down till I could not breathe. I had offered to pay for them, but where could I find the money?

I went to my friend Mrs. Lan and talked it over with her. She talked it over with Mrs. Reed. And Mrs. Reed went to talk it over with Miss Mason.

It happened one day that my neighbor's little boy saw some men carrying a procession of bridal presents, and in one of the carriers he recognized the young man who had stolen the glasses. He raised a great cry and the police took the young man in custody. And the young man confessed. I was so delighted that I went immediately to tell Miss Mason, and on the way met Mrs. Reed, who told me that she had arranged with Miss Mason for me to go back.

I went back and I said to Miss Mason, "It is all right. The boy has been caught."

And she said, "Have the glasses been found?" And I said that they had not but that the boy had been caught.

"Oh," said she, "is that poor boy in that very dirty prison? He must be let out at once." And she sent her cook to tell them to let him out immediately.

The boy came of a good family. He was the son of one who had been governor of Weihaiwei. So for his father's sake the matter was hushed up. They had become very poor and had no money to pay for the glasses or for anything else. The glasses were lost. The boy said he had put them in a crack in the wall. Who knows?

I worked for Miss Mason. When she was happy all was well. When she was not happy she would speak of the glasses.

I had nothing to do with my daughter. She had a child, another girl. Surely she was destined to ill fortune. When the child was four she died of scarlet fever and I was glad she died. To what family did she belong? Where would she fit in the pattern of life? Surely it was better that she died.

Then Chang Fa who owned a big truck garden by the sea came to me. He was an old neighbor from P'englai. He said, "Is she not your daughter?" So I went to see her and she came to see me, perhaps two or three times a year. But never have we been the same to each other as before.

My old uncle came to see me and I kept him with me a year, for I was fond of him. We had always got on, my old uncle and I. He had helped me in the days when I was without, and now that he was without I could share what little I had with him. He was eighty at this time and stayed with me a year.

My aunt had died, and the lame son-in-law had died. What little they had was gone. So my uncle's daughter went to the village outside the city to live with her eldest daughter and family. Then she married again and left her younger children with her daughter. When she got on the donkey to leave, the children clung to her and wept. When my uncle told me of this my heart turned over. How could she have borne it?

XVIII

MY SON IS STARTED IN LIFE

1921–1925

IT WAS time that my son should marry. Su Teh had been sent by the missionaries to Peking to school, and the other granddaughter was in Huanghsien, also in a a mission school. I rarely saw my daughter.

Through my friend Chang Fa, who owned the garden by the sea, I arranged for my son to marry Mei Yun, one of the girls in the school that my grandaughters had attended. My son was working for a friend he had known in the Customs, who had gone into business for himself, and his prospects seemed good. Mei Yun's brother had been prosperous and then gone bad. Some people can stand money and some cannot. To some more money than they have had is a poison. He had a good position with a lace company. Then he went into business for himself and learned to eat opium and failed. He failed for eighty thousand dollars, and so he ran away.

Mei Yun's mother had died and her father married again. Her stepmother was hard on the older children. They sent Mei Yun to the lace factory to make lace and would not let her go to school any more. So we set the time for the marriage and brought her home.

I had not seen my daughter for a long time. My friends urged me to let her know about the marriage. They said, "She is your daughter. You have only these two children." So I let my friends tell her, and she came home for the wedding and we were polite to one another.

But my temper is bad. Always is my temper bad. When

it came time to pay for the rickshamen who had brought the wedding attendants I paid them eight hundred cash each. It was no distance from one house to the other, only up the hill a short piece. But the ricksha pullers would not be content. So I asked them how much they wanted. They said two thousand. I said that was entirely too much and asked if the price had been stated. They said it had. I asked them who had stated, and they said that the other family had stated. So I told them to go to the other family. But my friends, and there were quite a few at the wedding, spoke up and begged me not to be angry. All knew my bad temper and they begged me not to go to the other house and quarrel with the family. They said, "It is a lifetime for your daughter-in-law. Do not let a few hundred cash spoil it."

So I paid the extra money. But when it became time for the third-day visit I sent her alone. I did not let my son go with her. He was but eighteen or nineteen. I was afraid that he would become embroiled in a quarrel beyond his years. And I did not let her go home again until the time for the regular New Year visit.

"What will you do," said Chang Fa, "when the child comes?" When the first child is born it is the duty of the husband to tell his wife's people.

"I will send a letter," I replied.

When the child was born, I was about to get a letter written when my daughter said, "Never mind. It is but a few steps. I will go." So she went and told them the news and the old man, Mei Yun's father, grunted.

"Good," he said. So that affair passed off. But not a thing did they send. In wealthy families the mother sends her daughter things enough to fill big red boxes carried between two men. You see them often going through the streets—all the things that a young mother and her child will need. And a poor family will send over a basket of things, clothes for the child and diapers, eggs and glutenous rice and red sugar for the mother. But they did not send a thing. And not only did they not send a thing but no one came to see her. This made her very sad and she felt differently toward her family.

The brother who had run away came back. He was poor and in need. I helped him with five or six dollars and helped him find a position. Then he quarreled with his father. I do not know what the quarrel was about but it was a very bitter quarrel. And the stepmother wanted to beat him but his father would not let her. She was so angered that she became ill and died of it. She was ill for three years. It became a consumption, and the feud in the family was worse as the years went on. But in the later years it was quiet.

Then one day the wife of Mei Yun's father's cousin, Ho Yun-fu, said to me, "Mei Yun's mother will soon die. Her little neck is no thicker than my wrist. Let Mei Yun go home to see the old woman. There is now no cause for feud."

Mei Yun was hurt because no one had come to see her when the baby was born, but after all the woman had tended her since she was five or six years old.

I said, "I shall not meddle with business that is not mine. If she wants to go home I shall not stop her. If she does not want to go I will not make her."

But the wife of Ho Yun-fu was not satisfied. "That is not the question. If you tell her to go she will go."

I answered, "How do I know that they will receive her after all this time? There might even be more trouble. If you wish, you may sound out the old people the next time you call. You might say in passing 'Now that our sister is so ill the daughter might be interested to know.' " And the wife of Ho Yun-fu said that she would sound them out.

When she spoke the father spat. "That generation born of rabbits," he said. "Those children of rabbits! What have I to do with them?" And so no one went from our family to see the death.

The old man was very stupid. When the old woman was dying he was very loud in his words, "Don't tell anyone. Don't send for the daughter. Don't send for the daughter-in-law." Since the son had run away the daughter-in-law had gone back to live with her own people in the country. He would not let them send for the widowed aunt, the widow of his uncle. And when he was asked what he would do with the children—there were four of them—he said that he would give them to their mother's sister to care for. So they took the coffin and buried her. Her sister came and wept at the grave and then she got on her donkey and rode away. There was no word of caring for the children.

He sent them to the home of a married niece, who kept them for a while. But she had children of her own. Who had time to care for four children, what with their soiling and their voiding? So he found a place for the girl as a betrothed wife in the husband's home. And her life was not easy, young as she was they had her make all the shoes for the family and do all the heavy work. I hear that they have since divorced her and a new mother-in-law has been found for her. The boys were put in the poorhouse. Chang Fa arranged it, I heard.

The old must think for the young. A family cannot be held together unless the older ones sacrifice for the young. Mei Yun's father's family is scattered. They live in six places. My family is all together, except for Su Teh, and she comes home in her vacations.

The summer my son was married Su Teh came back to see us. Now that I had my son settled for life I wished to provide her with a family, with people, that she might be placed in life. I spoke to Li Ching-shan, who had been her teacher in middle school. He was a son-in-law of my old friend Mrs. Lan. I spoke to him of my desire and asked if he knew of a suitable person. He said to give him time to think it over. The next day he came to me and said that Liu the tailor had a son whom we all knew and that it would be a good match. Also the family were willing. My granddaughter was well educated. Her English was very good, but in Chinese studies the boy was more proficient, so the match would not be unequal.

My heart was happy and I told Su Teh. But her face fell and she said, "I won't, I won't, I won't." So I told Mr. Li to let the matter drop. The Liu family did not like it much. It was a slight to turn them down after matters had gone that far. But I said that I would not constrain my granddaughter, that modern youth could not be forced. From that day to this I have never made any move to get her married. My daughter also took her part and said, "Would you also spoil her life as you have spoiled mine?"

But it is not well for a woman not to marry. When she is old she should have her people around her.

That winter I heard that my daughter and the man with whom she lived were planning to have his old uncle come to live with them. I knew that they had rented two rooms only and that my daughter and the man and the child slept in the outer room and that my granddaughter slept in the inner room. I asked my daughter where the old man would sleep and she said that he would sleep in the inner room. I was very angry. I asked her if she had so little knowledge of what was seemly as to let her daughter sleep on the same bed with a man. Even if he was seventy years old, still he was a man and she was now a great girl of fifteen. So she let me take the child home with me.

Nor was that convenient. I had but one room and on that one bed I had my daughter-in-law and her baby sleep. My son slept in the office where he worked. When he came home for the night, as he did twice a month on the first and the fifteenth, I went to the home of the Chang Fa family. An extra pallet could always be laid for an old woman like me. It was no easy thing for them to find room also for a girl of fifteen. But they were kind.

The old man never came after all, and my daughter said that I had taken her child away.

My younger granddaughter was attending the mission school. During the vacation Su Teh came home from Peking to see us. What she saw made her very unhappy. There were constant quarrels. So when Su Teh went back to Peking, the missionaries sent her sister to Huanghsien, near P'englai. They had also a school there. But even there she could not get away from her mother's shame.

The other girls would say to her, "Is not your mother a widow?"

"Yes," the child would say.

"But have you not a little sister?"

I scolded my granddaughter. I told her that she had no initiative. Could she not have said to them, "My father is dead so my mother has followed another husband." To follow a second husband was not a disgrace. It was not to one's honor but it was not a disgrace. But my younger granddaughter was a child. She could not think of these things and she fretted. She fretted so much that she became ill. They sent her back to the school in Chefoo. She had been there two or three days before I heard. As soon as I heard I went to the school to see her and I saw death in her face. I wrapped her in a quilt and took her to her mother's house. If she was to die she should die in her mother's house as was seemly. She was ill for ten or eight days longer and I did not see her or her mother. We met at her grave, her mother and I, and we spoke to each other. My granddaughter was buried in a fruit orchard on the side of the hill, and the blossoms were at their full.

It was my daughter who destroyed the life of her own child. The foreign doctors said that she died of typhoid fever, but I knew that she had died of shame and the anger that her mother put on her.

The man who had taken my son into business failed. For a year my son had no work. I wrote to my friends in Tsingtao and Peking. Mrs. Lan's son who was traveling for a lace company offered him work in India, but I would not let him go. The people in India are black and the place is hot. My son has never been strong. I said no. I wrote to my friends, and at last one of them found a place for him in Peking. It was to be an apprenticeship of three years as technician in a dentist's office. The dentist was a Shantung man also, and his wife was from P'englai. At the end of three years he would be a full technician. As an apprentice he would get his keep and money for shoes and shaves. Su Teh who had graduated and was teaching in a college in Peking sent us money to live on, his wife, the baby, and me.

My son was very homesick. He wrote to me, begging to come home. I wrote to him that he must stay. I said, "Can a woman, when it comes to her marriage day, say that she will not go to her mother-in-law? Are you not now a man with a family?" He stayed.

Then there was talk of a dental office to be opened in Chefoo by some friends of mine. They asked me if I would let my son join them. I sent for him. He started the day he got my letter. He would not wait even until the next week when the sister-in-law of his master was coming to Chefoo. He took the first train out of Peking and came.

He was very thin. He had been buying his food anywhere and he ate when he felt like it. He did not know how to spend money. He had always been under my direction. I said that he should not go back. But his master's father died and his master came back to Shantung to bury his father and passed through Chefoo. He came to see me. He said that my son should eat with his family and that on finishing his apprenticeship he should have thirty dollars a month. So I let my son go back. And then he gave him fifteen dollars only. If Su Teh had not helped we could not have lived.

It is in one's destiny. There are those who say that I should have stayed by my old man and not left him when he sold my daughter. Then I should have had more sons and older ones and have been better off now. There have been those who have begged and raised families to wealth.

There was a woman who had four sons. She begged and raised them. They all became mandarins. In Chefoo there was an old woman who used to beg through the streets of the city and sew on the beach for the sailors. In some way her son began to do a little peddling business by the sea and sell food to the sailors as they came ashore. Then he started a pawnshop. He became so wealthy that whatever he saw, anything new, he would buy for his mother. And when she remonstrated with him and said, "You should not have spent so much," he would say, "It did not cost much."

And always it was that it did not cost much.

His mother became ill. He knelt in the court and vowed a vow to go to T'aishan on a pilgrimage every year of her life. He vowed to burn incense there every year she lived, and to go by foot. She got well and he went every year, walking, carrying a load of incense on his back.

One year, as he walked, he met an old woman who said to him, "Why do you walk so far? The goddess of T'aishan is everywhere. Sometimes she is here and sometimes she is there. Where your incense catches fire there she is."

One day he went to the Temple of the Fire God and his incense caught fire. He called a meeting and formed a society. He set up a tablet and built a temple to the goddess of T'aishan. The people of Chefoo go there to worship in the Second Moon of every year.

It was summer and there were many visitors in Chefoo.

My friends knew that I wanted work, so they recommended me to the wife of the Russian consul. She had a guest from Tientsin staying with her. I said that I would go for thirty dollars a month, but she said that was too much. For people who lived in Chefoo I would work for fifteen or sixteen dollars a month. But for summer people, for a short time, with a chance of not getting work in the autumn, we must work for more. So I said that I would work for twenty-five but not less. They took me for twenty-five. The baby came to me immediately. He had refused to let the other amah touch him. He screamed when she came near but he liked me.

The Russians are easy to work for. Also they eat better than any other kind of foreigner. Mrs. Yardley was English. Always with her it was the same kind of food, a chicken roasted whole or a piece of beef roasted and some boiled vegetables. They had morning tea in bed before they got up. Their breakfast was always the same—some bread and butter and jam, some gruel, and a glass of milk. In the middle of the morning there were tea and cakes and in the middle of the afternoon tea and cakes. They could not get away from cakes. But the Russians ate many things. They seemed to have all the things that foreigners ate and the things that we ate also. Their women could go into the kitchen and cook for themselves and do it well. The mother-in-law of a Russian woman for whom I washed used to go into the kitchen and cook. She would make pelmeni, something like our chiaotze, and noodles. When they were made, she would lay aside a couple of dumplings or a bit of noodles for me. She would say, "Here, take this and try it."

When madam went back to Tientsin she wanted to take me with her. I said that I could not go. She said that she gave me good wages and the work was not too heavy and why should I not go with her. I told her that was all true and that I would like to go with her, and that my son was in Peking, so that I would like even more to go with her but that I could not. She was angry with me and went away. But I could not go. My daughter-in-law was going to have a baby in the Ninth or Tenth Moon, and I could not leave her or take her in her condition on a journey to a strange place. Also I was having a lawsuit. I had lent a hundred and fifty dollars to a man and he would not repay, so I had gone to law. The case was to be tried in the Eighth Moon.

But for that work of two months I had no regular work from the time my son left. Those were hard years. I sewed and washed, when I was called, and made five or six dollars a month. With these years of idleness and the three years when my son had no work all my savings, about three hundred dollars, were used up.

My son went to Peking in the First Moon. It was then that the lawsuit started and it was not ended until the Ninth Moon.

All that year the affair dragged on. I had lent the money to the washman, Kao, the one with pockmarks who had a shop on the North River and two sons in the Weiling School where my son had studied. He borrowed money from me at two per cent a month, three dollars a month for three years. Then it became difficult for him to pay, it hurt a little to take out the money for me each month. He claimed that he had lent the money to others and they could not re-pay me.

Everyone knew that my son was a quiet man. I sent him to ask for the money and tell the man we would sue if he did not give it.

Kao said to my son, "I am not afraid. Then sue."

My son went to Peking and I went to see Kao. He did not like that. "Where is your son?" he said.

"That matters not to you. It is with me that you are

to do business. The affair started with me. Let it end with me."

At last he said, "Go to court. I cannot pay."

And I answered, "Whom shall I accuse? We have been friends." So I went to court and accused him of not paying his just debts. But afterward he was sorry and wanted to get middlemen and talk the matter to a settlement. But it was too late. I had already spent money to buy the official paper on which the complaint was made out and paid the fee for filing the complaint. All three families went to court, mine, the washman's, and that of my friend who had been middleman in the borrowing.

When we sat in the court, day after day waiting our turn, we saw many other cases—adultery, opium, robbery, murder, a sister who had injured a brother, and an opium smuggler. She was an old woman.

The judge asked, "Why do you sell opium? Do you not know it is illegal?"

"Yes."

"Why do you sell it?"

"I have no other way to eat. If I should try to find an old mate no one would have me even for a latrine."

"Hai! You addled egg. Roll," said the magistrate.

In all I went ten times to court and it took most of the year before the matter was settled, but I got the money.

The baby was born in the Ninth Moon and it was a boy.

XIX

PEIPING

1928-1934

WHEN the second child was in his third year and my son had finished his apprenticeship he came and took us to Peiping.* I did not want to go. I did not want to leave my friends and the life I knew, but my son was in Peiping and he was all I had left. My daughter and the man she lived with had gone to Shanghai. He had a job as a cook in a boardinghouse for sailors and was making good money. He contracted for the food. My granddaughter, Su Teh, was teaching in the college in Peiping and making good money. She sent us the money for our journey to Peiping. My son's master had raised his wages to twenty dollars a month, so we set up our house in Peiping and there was peace for several years.

But always in my heart I was thinking of my daughter in Shanghai and longing for her. She should be with her own people and not with that strange man. I told Su Teh and urged her to go to her mother in Shanghai and to see how she was. I said to Su Teh, "If your mother wishes to come back to us we will be very glad."

Also I had heard that the man was tiring of her and paying more attention to his other family. My daughter was not as young as she had been and with the years she had put on much flesh. She had always been fat but now, they said, she was very fat. When I had seen Su Teh off on the train I prayed all the time that she was on the way

* The government changed the name of Peking to Peiping after the 1927 revolution.

—I prayed that my daughter might come back to me in peace. The foreigners and the Christians have their gods they pray to and we have ours. Little did I know when I was praying with such joy in my heart what trouble I was bringing upon us.

Su Teh wrote that the man had no job and that my daughter was unhappy and would come home to us. I rented a house in a larger court. I rented three rooms so that she could have one to herself. It was a larger house than my son and I could afford, but Su Teh had promised to help with the rent. Also she came and helped us to make ready.

My daughter came. Never a moment from the time she arrived did we have peace. Always there were quarrels or bitter silences. I had ruined her life in a hundred ways, she said.

Truly my destiny is not a good one. I was not born at an auspicious time. The eight words of my birth time are not good ones. My husband spoiled my youth, my son-in-law my middle years, and now it is my daughter who makes my old age unhappy. Truly in her younger days she was not as she is now. In these later years she has ever gone further from me.

Always she blames me that the spring of her life was not realized. Truly her youth was a hard one. There were times when she was hungry and times when she was cold and her husband was not a person. But she holds against me most bitterly the days when she cooked in the early mornings for her father that he might do his peddling.

Even with an extra room there was now not space enough in our home. Always my daughter was complaining. She told of all she had done for me. Once, in the early days in Peiping when my son was not earning enough for us to eat, Su Teh had written to her mother and told her of our need. My daughter sent money two or three times, forty or fifty dollars each time. She now told us of that. She told of the clothes she had sent to her daughter when her daughter was in college and that her daughter did not wear them. It was a cause for complaint that she would not wear them. But my granddaughter did not like the same colors or materials that her mother liked and she could not wear the clothes her mother sent her. They were of silk such as Shanghai women wore—bright colors and large figures. Su Teh had good taste and could not wear them. They were suitable for a wife in a home but not for a teacher in a school. My daughter told of the money she had sent us and of her own hard youth. Never once did she speak of my hard life or of her brother's hard youth.

My granddaughter lived in the college but she came often to see us. She was always a good girl. Even the once that she hurt me was not her fault. She saw how things were and she said that it would be better if we were to live apart. Of that I would not hear. I was afraid that my daughter would go back to that man. If she wanted a man why could she not have picked one without a wife?

And so one day when I was not at home they moved out. My granddaughter found a house for her mother and helped her to move out. When I was not at home they moved away. They did not tell me what they were doing. When I came home she was gone. They had left a message with my son's wife. That was all. They had left a message with the mother of my grandson.

I went to the wife of my son's employer. She was also an old friend from P'englai. And I said to her, "What do my children mean by treating me so?"

She said many words to comfort me. Then she said, "Your daughter told me that she was not deserting you —that she would send you ten dollars a month."

Then I saw her meaning and it was clear to me and a

great anger surged in my heart. Not for years had I been so enraged. I went to find Su Teh. I would not enter the fine house in which she was staying, an old servant woman like me. I sat on the steps and waited. They said that she had gone for a walk. Perhaps she had gone to see her mother. I sat on the steps and waited. Then she came.

"Grandmother, what are you doing here? Come in." But I would not.

"I am not fit to come into the grand house and see your grand friends. What I have to say I will say to you here." But she continued to beg me to come in and then she pulled five dollars—no, it was six—out of her pocket and tried to give them to me.

Even the heart of my granddaughter had been poisoned by my daughter. My rage became too strong. I turned and started away. Su Teh called after me, "Grandmother, I will come to see you tonight."

She had been to see her mother and they had talked me over between them. My daughter could not write a letter. She told her daughter to write a letter for her, and in that letter were written all my sins. Then she sent it to my son. He opened and read it. He did not want to read it to me but I made him. Then I told him that he must write a letter to them for me. He did not want to write it but I told him that he must. He had brought the letter home with him after work. My granddaughter has said that she would come that evening, but she had not come and the letter said that she would not.

I told my son what to write. I told of her childhood when I had begged and starved for her, and of her youth when I fought for her and suffered all manner of hardship for her.

While my son was writing Su Teh came. If she had not come that evening I doubt if I should ever have forgiven her. She came. She stood in the court. She was afraid to come in, for she heard the angry tones of my voice as I told my son what to write. The neighbors gathered round her. There were three families in the court. She said that she would go home, but they told her that I was not angry, that I was hurt. So she came in and she wept and I wept. What else was there for us to do?

For weeks I would take no money from her. For months I would not see my daughter.

Su Teh came often to see us. One day when she was leaving she put six dollars in my hand. "Not for you," she said, "but for the children, to buy them some sweets." The money was for the children of my son. She is a good girl, my granddaughter.

Then my daughter began to come back to see me. But always when she comes there is unrest. We had nothing to say to each other that did not lead to quarrels. In her presence I am dumb. My words are pressed back into me. When I see her coming I get out the chessboard. We play a game together. What else can we do?

It is of no use to be envious of one's destiny. The anger born in the heart leads to no good and makes for illness. Even if I am not dressed as those above me, why should I fear their ridicule? I have not stolen. I have not borrowed their money. I have not committed adultery. I feel that I am as good as they. It is not so with my daughter. It is the envy in her heart that corrodes.

She also makes Mei Yun unhappy. Mei Yun is gentle and takes things as they come, but my daughter makes her unhappy also. The landlord sold the house in which we were living, so we had to move. Mei Yun said, "Let us not tell the sister." By rights, as my daughter, she should be told that we were moving so that she could come home and help. That would be the right thing. But I understood my daughter-in-law and so I agreed. But my daughter heard and came anyway. We were placing the beds in the new house. My daughter came in and helped. She put a bed under a beam. She said, "We are not afraid to sleep under a beam."

My daughter-in-law said nothing, but her face became long and heavy and she moved the bed. For the rest of the day she went about her tasks with her face long and heavy. When I saw this my heart also became heavy. The anger rose in it. I have always been a woman of anger but now it was anger that I could not let out. What could I say? I pressed the anger into my heart. My daughter, my daughter-in-law, and the children were around me. I said nothing but I became ill. I was ill for ten days. Truly to suppress anger is not good.

My daughter comes home on Sundays. Her brother is at home on that day. It is her duty to the family to come and see us, but it does not make us happy. But I dare not quarrel more with her for there is always the fear in my heart that she will go back to that man. He has lost his job in Shanghai, they tell me, and has gone back to Chefoo. When she says that she does not like Peiping and will go back to Chefoo a cold fear settles at my heart.

I did not like Peiping. I wanted to go back to Chefoo. First I said, "I will not go while my granddaughter is away." Her college sent her for a year to America to study in one of the big schools. I said I would wait until she got back from her studies abroad. Then I would deliver her mother to her. My son is now independent. He can make enough to support his family. He is independent and does not need me. As soon as he was making enough to support himself and his wife and his children I ceased to control his wages. I gave them over to his wife. I planned that when Su Teh came back from America I would take myself back to Chefoo or to P'englai where my friends could be around me and I could live out the few days that remain to me. There, with my friends, I could talk over the past that we all know. Truly all my life I have spent thinking of my family. The time is soon here when they need me no more but for this year they still needed me and I had to stay.

I said that with what money I had saved I would go to Shantung to live. I would go to P'englai and see the places of my youth. I would look up the few old friends that are left. I would go to Chefoo and take a small room there and end my days among my own friends. But first I had to wait until my granddaughter came back. We were both afraid that my daughter would go back to that man.

XX

THE FAMILY ESTABLISHED

1934–1937

MY GRANDDAUGHTER, Su Teh, came back from America and was even better to us than before. She had a good position in the college and lived in the hall where the women teachers lived. She made much money and was very generous. Every Sunday she came to see us and brought things for the children and helped with the tuition for the children of my son.

Su Teh gave money to her mother each month and her mother was content. She played majong with her friends and they called her Mrs. Li. She dressed like a woman of leisure and lived like a woman of leisure. Perhaps she felt that the autumn of her life was not as bitter as the spring.

Then I became ill. One side of my face would not work, one of my arms and one of my legs would not work. It must have been caused by the anger that had been stored up in me, that each week I kept back, when my daughter came to see me, and did not let out. It must have been this stored-up anger, for there was no special anger that brought it on. One morning I could not get up.

When I was ill my daughter came to see me. She spent much money on me, and so did my son. My daughter stayed with me all the time and she gave me the medicines the doctors ordered, and it was very expensive medicine. She got the best doctors in the city for me, even the one from the West City that all said was the best in town and skilled in acupuncture. We had others also but he was the best.

My children gave me the medicines that the doctors ordered and I got well. Some of the medicine cost as much as three dollars a pill, and my daughter did not begrudge it to me. My granddaughter also came often to see me. She brought a foreign doctor to see me. Truly I was well cared for.

So I knew that my daughter loved me in spite of all. We can now see each other without quarreling but we bicker. I think that we will always bicker. She does not come too often.

I got well and could walk with a cane and my face was as it had been. But I had not as much strength as I had before.

I went to Chefoo to see my old friends and to sell my furniture. I stayed with the Chang Fa family and saw all my old friends. I had a very good time, but I found that I could not rest my heart in Chefoo. I was thinking about the grandchildren. I wanted to see them. I was worried about them. I thought about them all the time.

Now I have been to Chefoo and am content. I will stay with my children and my grandchildren. It is good to have one's children. It is good when one is old to be surrounded by one's own people.

My son wanted to buy a house. He said it would be well for us to have our own place. It is seemly for people to live in the house they own. We found a house for sale. It had a cement floor and plaster ceiling. It was hard and I felt that I was in prison. My son said it was clean but to me it was hard. I am used to the paper ceilings and brick floors. Nor was it harmonious. I could not have lived there. There were three north rooms and six south rooms. The houses were not set as they should be in the courts. One house of three rooms was in a small court off the main court. I think it must have been part of a larger house onto which some builder added the extra rooms. There was no rhythm nor harmony. It would not be good for our destinies, the eight characters could not agree in such a place. There was also a bitter water well outside the gate.

I am now happy and contented, and settled in Peiping I can still sew for the children and make gifts for my friends. I can still prepare the special foods, the tsengtze for the Fifth Moon festival and the nien kao for New Year's. The grandchildren like the *paotze*, the steamed meat dumplings, I make for their birthdays.

The children of my son are good children. The two oldest are going to school. They bring home their report cards and they have done well. The third has been sick. He is a spoiled child. We are going to have trouble with him. His father loves him best of all. He looks like my family, like the Hsu family. I love all my grandchildren, but if I should say which one I loved the best I should say that I love the oldest boy. He was the first boy. My daughter-in-law loves the baby the best. That is always the way with mothers. The children know all this and talk about it, and they say that their aunt loves the little girl the best. So there is a grown person to love each child.

My daughter still lives alone but she has taken a house near mine. She lives alone, so the little girl, my son's daughter, goes to spend the nights with her. My daughter is still a fool but we do not quarrel now, we only bicker. Perhaps we do quarrel a little sometimes, but I have learned to let things pass that I would never have let pass before.

We have a happy home. My son and my daughter-in-law are good to me and they are good to each other. The children fuss sometimes, but that is the way with children, and our house is small. My son is getting forty-five dollars a month now and we have enough to eat and to wear and we are warm in the winter, but our house is small.

My health is good. I can move my arms and legs. I can sew, but my strength does not last. I get tired more

LAO T'AI T'AI LEARNS SOMETHING ABOUT AMERICA

quickly than I did before and cannot sew now for as many hours. It even tires me now to go to the theater or to listen to the storytellers at the market. I still go sometimes for an hour or two, but then the backless benches make me tired. They tell me that I am old and cannot expect to be otherwise. But I do not feel old, and in my dreams I am always entirely young. I dream of the days in P'englai. I am with my mother or my brother. I am fighting with the husband of my daughter or I am talking with my uncle. But always I am young and vigorous.

My granddaughter, Su Teh, is a successful woman. But she has not married. I tell my granddaughter she should marry. She says that marriage is not necessary to working for the country. That is new talk. We all know that the family is more important than anything else. Every woman must have a husband and children. How can there be a country if there are no families and children?

My granddaughter is thirty-five and she has not married. I went to her teacher, her old friend. I said, "Can you not do something about it? Do you not know one of those with whom she works, an educated man with whom she can talk? Could you not arrange a match for my granddaughter before it is too late? She should have her family. She should have her people around her."

Life must go on. The generations stretch back thousands of years to the great ancestor parents. They stretch for thousands of years into the future, generation upon generation. Seen in proportion to this great array, the individual is but a small thing. But on the other hand no individual can drop out. Each is a link in the great chain. No one can drop out without breaking the chain. A woman stands with one hand grasping the generations that have gone before and with the other the generations to come. It is her common destiny with all women.

XXI

THE JAPANESE COME AGAIN

1937–1938

M Y SON and my granddaughter Su Teh talked of the Japanese and of the power they were gaining and their desire to take over more of China each year. It is not reasonable for the Japanese to take land that is not theirs. It is not the way of those who understand. It is the way of robbers and of such as should be removed from among mankind. Surely, I said, they will not come into China, into a country that is not theirs, and take what is not theirs. But my son and my granddaughter said that they would come and make us much trouble. Su Teh said that we should think of what we should do when they came, if they came. She said that she would not stay in Peiping if the Japanese became masters. She and many of her friends had decided to leave Peiping if the Japanese came, and go somewhere to work for our country. That was new talk which I did not understand, but my granddaughter is a good girl. Why should she leave this good job to go where people do not know her and where there are none of her own people?

My son read the paper to me each evening. I began to see what Su Teh was talking about. The paper told each day of the Japanese. My son said that each day they came closer and that each day they took more of that which belonged to China. The feeling these actions of the Japanese gave me was like the feeling on board ship—the fear and the uncertainty.

Then silver became of no use. It became waste material.

My son said that if anyone bought any silver he would be imprisoned. If silver was taken to the silversmith it could not be used. The smiths had orders to use only one third silver in all ornaments. The old people say that it is no use to think too far ahead. Destiny is determined in ways we do not know. When my granddaughter brought those dollars to me I rang them each one and kept only the best. Now the silver dollar is of no use and pieces of paper have taken their place. That is not according to reason. Silver will always be worth more than paper. Banks come and go. I have my little hoard. I kept two hundred dollars hidden in my room, in case we must fly in the night, and I asked my friend, the teacher of my granddaughter, to put some of my savings, three hundred dollars, into the American bank. In that way I will have some money if the Japanese come and take what we have at home.

The war came nearer. I remembered what my son had read about a little country where the people are all black and have no big guns. And every day the airplanes from a country in Europe went over and dropped bombs on them. The Japanese have come nearer each month and they are more arrogant each day. They ride in big motor cars and, my son says, the decisions made in the city are their decisions.

One year was like the next, except that the children were promoted from one grade to another, and, my son said, the Japanese came closer, taking each year more of the land belonging to China. For people living as we did, there was not much difference. It was only in the talk of my son and my granddaughter that I knew of any difference—and things became more expensive to buy.

Then one day we gave my son his breakfast as usual. It was summer and we had daylight to cook his breakfast. He started to work, but before we could get the breakfast things cleared away he was back again. He said that our soldiers would not let him cross the main street, so he could not get to work. He said the streets were empty, as in the middle of the night, and the soldiers stood guard with long bayonets. We stayed inside our gate and all the people went into their houses and shut their gates. When soldiers fight that is all the people can do. The city was quiet; never have I heard the city so quiet.

Every morning my son went to see if he could cross the main street, and on the third day the soldiers let him cross. They let us cross between sunrise and sunset, and those that brought vegetables from the truck gardens outside the city came again, and we had food to eat.

Then the guns began to roar. They roared all day and all night. There was fighting, they said, in the south of the city, in the South Barracks. The stories of the fighting were thick like snow in the winter. We gathered in the side streets in knots and told each other what we heard, and we were afraid.

We were proud of our people. They told of one boy outside the Anting Gate. He had a bloody sword. He had killed eight Japanese with his sword. It was dripping with blood. He waved it over his head and sang a song from the romance of the *Three Kingdoms*, and fell dead. He was a brave boy. Our men are each equal to eight Japanese. But the Japanese have guns and airplanes and we have only swords.

There were refugees coming into the city. In our street a family from a village outside the South City came to some relatives and stayed a few days. They had not much to tell. They had heard the guns roaring and had packed their things and left. They had not seen any Japanese. They heard the firing and ran. My son says there are many refugees in the city, and his master belongs to a committee to feed them. My granddaughter says that they come to the hospital.

We were all frightened but where should we run? We could have run from here, but my son says that it would have been as bad in Shantung. We decided we might as well stay here. We said, "If it is in our fate to live we will live, if to die we will die." No one can escape his fate. When the Japanese shelled P'englai, Old Chang, the dirt cart pusher, took his wife and two children and hid in the cave on the P'englai bluff. He stepped out of the cave. A shell struck him and killed him. His home was not touched. He was one of the two or three to die. We can but go into our house and stay.

A policeman went to the school and told the children not to talk too freely and not to linger on the streets after the classes were over.

The Japanese will not be content until we are like Manchuria. The teacher of my granddaughter says that when they get North China they will try to take South China, and then they will try to eat up America. They want all beneath the heavens.

Only the Son of Heaven could hold such power and he receives it from his ancestor Heaven. Only he who held the Mandate of Heaven could have the power. The sign of the power, the token of the mandate, is in the imperial seal.

The Japanese want all that is under heaven. That they cannot have. But the great seal is lost. The seal is gone, no one knows where. When the Empress Dowager fled from the foreigners in 1900, at the time of the Boxer trouble, she took it with her but did not bring it back. She lost it, perhaps, in the plains of Mongolia. Without the Mandate of Heaven and the seal there can be no power. There is no great Nine Tiger Seal for the Chief General. How can the Japanese capture the earth? I have seen the great seal cases in the Forbidden City, a room full of boxes, all empty.

There was a great thunderstorm one night, and the thunderbolt knocked off the corner of the tower over the

Chi Hua Gate. An old tablet was seen which had been buried by our fathers in the tower. The inscription was published in the papers. My son read it to me. The verses were an old prophecy and they said that the year of fulfillment has come.

Surely it is good to be able to read. The old people told us about what happened, what they learned when they went to the market places. The young people read to us from the newspapers.

It is not easy to understand prophecies. This prophecy is a poem. It talks of things that will happen, and some say that the time it is talking of is now. It talks of foreign people coming to our land but it talks also of foreign people leaving our land.

There are two stanzas to the poem. The first no one can translate, because only the gods know the meaning. The second is like this:

"Emperor of Heaven, Emperor of Earth, and Emperor
    of People,
Three emperors' heads shine with red light.
Fifteenth of the Eighth Moon will have no moon,
Fifteenth of Ninth Moon will reach the ocean."

This, all the people said, was to prophesy that by the Ninth Moon the Japanese would be driven into the ocean. The fifteenth of the Eighth Moon that had no moon was referring to the time in the Yuan dynasty when the people each killed the Mongol in his home and so drove the Mongols out of China. The message which told of the time for the killing was hid in the moon cakes, and so on that fifteenth of the Eighth Moon there was no moon for the enemy.

The Japanese came. My son said they marched into the city through the South Gate as the Chinese soldiers marched out through the West and Northwest Gates. They took over the yamen and the barracks. The Japanese became masters of the city as the Manchus did before and as the Mongols did many hundreds of years before that.

There is an old prophecy, the T'ui Pei T'u, worked out by two Immortals. It says that in the end Peiping will be destroyed by a steel wind air. I am afraid that it means Peiping will be bombed by the Japanese. My friends and the friends of my son tell me that the Japanese like Peiping and want to keep it whole for themselves so there is no danger of their destroying it. But I am afraid. It seems to me that the coming of the Japanese is not the end. There may be more. But it is of the present time the prophecy speaks. The beginning words are:

"The dragon has lost his teeth
Both men and women have cut their hair."

The dynasty has gone and there is no new one; the teeth of the dragon have dropped out. Hair, part of the body given us by our ancestors, is cut, even by women.

The old people say that in every life there is bitterness and there is happiness. There is good and there is bad. We say that we cannot bear our troubles but when we get to them we bear them.

The old people tell us that there must be trouble in every life. I had my personal troubles in the early part of my life and now there is peace in my own life but for my daughter. In the land, however, there was peace in my early years. There was peace in the land from the Taiping Rebellion to the present. I was born after the Taiping Rebellion was over. The old people and the young people were still talking of it as I grew up. It was fresh to them, but it has passed. The little wars do not count. There are always little wars on the borders of the land. But now, my son and my granddaughter say, there is a big war in the land and there is trouble for us all.

Perhaps it is a new dynasty come to rule us, but Su Teh does not agree. She says that we must fight, that we must not give in to the Japanese. How can we fight? I do not understand such matters. The Mongols came and conquered us, but we drove them out. The Manchus came and conquered us, but now they are part of us. We cannot now tell the difference between the Manchu and the Chinese.

Perhaps the Mandate of Heaven has passed to the Japanese. No one knows where the great seal is now. Some say that the Japanese got it. If the Japanese got it they will have the Mandate of Heaven and we should listen to them as our new masters.

My granddaughter says no. She says we must resist and not have any masters. She says that the land must be governed by the people of the land. She says that a new China is being born. I do not understand such words. That is new talk. How can people govern a land? Always there has been a Son of Heaven who is the father and mother of the people. If he is a bad father and mother, the Mandate of Heaven passes from him and a new emperor comes, one whom Heaven has chosen.

My granddaughter helps her friends in the hospital to get supplies to the guerrillas in the hills. She will not tell me about it. She says it is dangerous for me to know. Every day we hear the guns roaring outside the city. Every day we hear the bombs falling and bursting on the hills where the guerrillas have their camps. They tell us that the old temples where the guerrillas stay are being destroyed by the bombs. My granddaughter says that the guerrillas move on to another temple or village, that the Japanese bomb the rocks in the hills and waste their ammunition.

But the Japanese must sometimes bomb people also or why should the guerrillas need medical supplies?

My granddaughter tells me that a new China is building, that the guerrillas will work with the people and win the war. I don't know. It seems better to me that we should not have war and destruction. Our ancestors changed their dress for the Manchu invaders but did not change themselves. We are Chinese and will always be Chinese. They cannot change us. But if we are dead we are dead.

I tell my son to do his work. That is what we Chinese have always done. We work for our families and we live.

Su Teh is planning to go to Free China. I tell her it is dangerous to go through the Japanese lines. I am afraid. She says that she is afraid also but that she must go.

What can we do? The children, my grandchildren, the boys and the girl, are too young to make a march or to suffer the hardships of a journey. Who are there in other provinces who know us, who will give work to my son to feed the mouths of these children? My daughter is too fat and weak to make the journey. We will stay here and win through if the fates are with us. If the fates are not with us we will perish together, the whole family. If we live, we live, and that is good for China also.

Two Japanese living on our street went to the country one day and did not return, nor did the Chinese who went with them. Their families moved away, and we all kept inside our gates. Su Teh says their bodies were found outside the city. The guerrillas had killed them.

Every day the guns roar. My granddaughter tells me we will have no peace until the Japanese are driven from the land. I tell her that we will live here, my son and his wife and the children and my daughter also. We will live here as long as there is work for my son. His master is good and his work is such that all men need it whether they be Chinese or Japanese. We can manage somehow to live. The schools are better here. If there is no work we will, one family, die together. I do not believe in families separating.

I do not like my granddaughter's going away. I am afraid for her. Last New Year her mother was steaming bread. The loaves blew up and burst. They spread open like pomegranates. What happens to the bread at New Year's tells the fates for the year. Her fortune was burst, and in her fortune is bound that of her daughter.

One night I dreamed that a man on the street tried to seize one of the grandchildren, either Su Teh, the daughter of my daughter, or Shao Lan, the daughter of my son. I ran, and the man seized me by the hair. I went to the house and knocked at the door. My daughter came to the door and went with us also. All three of us were to be taken to the hall of justice, to the yamen of the district magistrate. Then my daughter wanted to get out of the trouble and tried to leave us. But I said that we must all go together, to explain our side of the matter, to give our reasons.

This was a dream of death, such as I had dreamed for the old grandfather many years ago. One of us was being taken to the judgment after death. One of us three must die. Perhaps it means that my daughter will die. Perhaps it means that my granddaughter, Su Teh, will die at the hands of the Japanese. Truly I am afraid to have her go. I hope that the dream is for me. Soon I will die anyway.

Again I dreamed that two cats were under the cooking stove. When the fire was built, the smoke drove one of the cats away. I knew it was a sign that one of the two who were tigers, who were born in the tiger year, would have trouble. When I dreamed this dream I did not think it would be Su Teh. I was always telling Mao Chia, the second grandson, to be careful, to wear more clothes when it was cold. He also was born in the tiger year.

My granddaughter came to say good-by. She brought us the things she had in her rooms. She said it would be many years before she would need them again. She told us that she had put her savings in the hands of my son to be used for her mother and for us. She said that she would send us money if she could. Truly she is filial. She said that one must be good to one's family, but that one must work for the country also.

She would not tell us when she was leaving or which way she would go. She said that she would wear the clothes of an amah, or those of a peasant woman, and that she would be safe. The Japanese do not stop the peasants, she said. How can Su Teh, who is an educated woman, whose hands are soft, dress like a peasant and not be found out? I am afraid for her.

I would like to go and see her off. But she says that is not possible. No one must know when and how she goes. The tears ran down her cheeks and the tears ran down my cheeks and the cheeks of my daughter, her mother.

I am afraid for my granddaughter but I am not afraid for myself. I am an old woman. What does it matter what happens to me? I am afraid for my grandchildren. But while there is life in me and in my son we will work for these children.